A Quick Guide to
32 Organizational Development Tools for Leaders
Volume 2

Keith B. Grant, PhD and Melvin Rusher, PhD

Keith B. Grant Press—Novi, MI
ISBN: 979-8-218-57498-7
Library of Congress Control Number: 2024920989
Title: *A Quick Guide to 32 Organizational Development Tools for Leaders*
Author: Keith B. Grant, PhD and Melvin Rusher, PhD
Digital distribution | 2024
Paperback | 2024

Dedication

For *Patricia A. Grant*

Introduction

No matter how carefully plans are made and tasks delegated, no complex organizational system can ever be perfect. A few problems are inevitable. To some degree, your success as a person, will depend on how quickly you can cut through the symptoms, get at the real cause of problems, and make timely and accurate decisions. Problem solving is more than an exercise in logic and deduction. The real cause of these problems may be disguised by many complex human and organizational factors. This resource treats the problem solving and decision-making procedures in a context of human relations. It shows how to cope with error and imperfection, look for real cause, create alternatives and make decision available.

This book provides useful explanations and tips on how to use the 32 problem solving tools. People often treat the symptoms of a problem rather than the cause. Your job is to weed through symptoms and find the real cause. This is sometimes difficult because you maybe the cause.

Introduction to the Toolkit

How to use the Problem-Solving Toolkit

The Problem-Solving Toolkit is a resource for leaders and employees. It provides a variety of tools that can assist in solving problems, developing change solutions and planning the successful implementation of those solutions. This toolkit contains Leading Change and Value Stream Mapping tools with process suggestions and tips for using them effectively.

The following is summarized for each tool:

- **What is it?** — provides a brief description of the tool
- **Why use it?** — notes the main reasons for applying the tool
- **Steps** — describes suggested steps
- **Tips** — provides some suggestions on how to use the tool

Finding a Tool

If...	Then...
you know the tool you need	use the Index (Page 88) to locate it. The tools are in alphabetical order.
you are not sure which tool to use	• use the Tool Selection Chart (Page vii) to determine the tool that would best meet your needs. The Tool Selection Chart organizes the tools by typical situations in which you may find yourself working, such as working with ideas, problems, stakeholder/participants or implementation **or** • use the chart at the beginning of each section (Pages ix, 6, 44, 62, 77) to view the tools in that section, situations in which to use the tool and the page on which the tools are found.

Tool Selection Chart

The Tool Selection Chart organizes the tools by typical situations in which you may find yourself working, such as working with ideas, problems, stakeholder/participants or implementation.

Working with Business Plans (Page ix)	Analyze	Prioritize	Track Results	Page #
Find It and Fix It	◆	◆		1
Business Plan Deployment	◆	◆	◆	4

Working with Ideas (Page 6)	Generate/ Group/Sort	Define/Clarify/Scope	Determine Action	Page #
15 Words		◆		7
Backward Imaging		◆		9
Brainstorming	◆			11
Circles of Control, Influence, Concern	◆			13
Diagnostic Questions and *Leading Change* Profile		◆	◆	15
Dot Voting			◆	21
Elevator Speech		◆		23
Fist to Five & Thumbs Up			◆	26
Force Field Analysis	◆			27
Gallery of Issues	◆		◆	29
In the Frame / Out of the Frame		◆		32
Is / Is Not		◆		33
More of / Less Of		◆		34
Payoff Matrix	◆		◆	36
Purpose Statement		◆	◆	38
SIPOC	◆	◆	◆	39
Threats versus Opportunities		◆		42

Working with Problems/Waste (Page 44)	Identify	Analyze	Eliminate	Page #
5 Step (5S)	◆	◆	◆	45
5 Why Problem Solving	◆	◆		49
COMMWIP	◆	◆	◆	52
Fishbone	◆	◆		57
Pareto Principle		◆		59

Working with Stakeholders/Participants (Page 62)	Identify	Attitudes	Behaviors	Page #
Attitude Curve	◆	◆		63
Leaders Matrix			◆	65
Participant and Leadership Panel Lists	◆			70
Stakeholder Analysis	◆		◆	74

Working with Action Items/Implementation (Page 77)	Define	Execute	Accountability	Page #
Action Register	◆	◆	◆	78
Communications Action Plan	◆	◆		81
RASIC	◆		◆	83
SOS and JES for Non-manufacturing Processes	◆	◆	◆	86

Working With Business Plans

When you need to:	See this tool:	Page:
Develop a business plan and identify appropriate change tools to achieve business results	Find It and Fix It	1
Set targets, integrate plans and focus the organization to achieve objectives and manage change	Business Plan Deployment (BPD)	4

Find It and Fix It

What is it? **Find It and Fix It**, originally called "The Performance Delivery Process," is used to aid leaders and organizations in focusing on the achievement of business objectives, using the right tools applied to the right ideas to achieve business results. It begins with an analysis of current business processes within a given organization and ends with results that improve these processes and achieve business objectives. It is most effective when it is championed by senior leadership and flows down through the various levels of an organization.

Why use it?
1. Provides a standardized process to understand the current business and achieve improvements in the future
2. Seeks the input and good ideas of all people across an organization
3. Applies effective tools to actual business problems/improvement initiatives
4. Provides a plan and a tracking mechanism for achieving business objectives

Steps:
1. Identify Functional Business Objective(s)
2. Identify major Work Streams and the corresponding business objective value for each
3. Identify Processes utilized within each Work Stream and the associated business objective value/relative proportion for each
4. Allocate annual Business Objective Target by Work Stream
5. Identify improvement ideas/opportunities
6. Create Prioritized Project Plan / BPD
7. Scope each idea on the Project Plan / BPD
8. Execute each viable idea using the appropriate tool (Value Stream Mapping, Leading Change, Just Do it, etc.)
9. Create an implementation plan and monitor implementation for each executed idea
10. Regularly check the sufficiency of the overall Project Plan and determine countermeasures/ next steps based on actual results

Find It & Fix It Driving Great Results

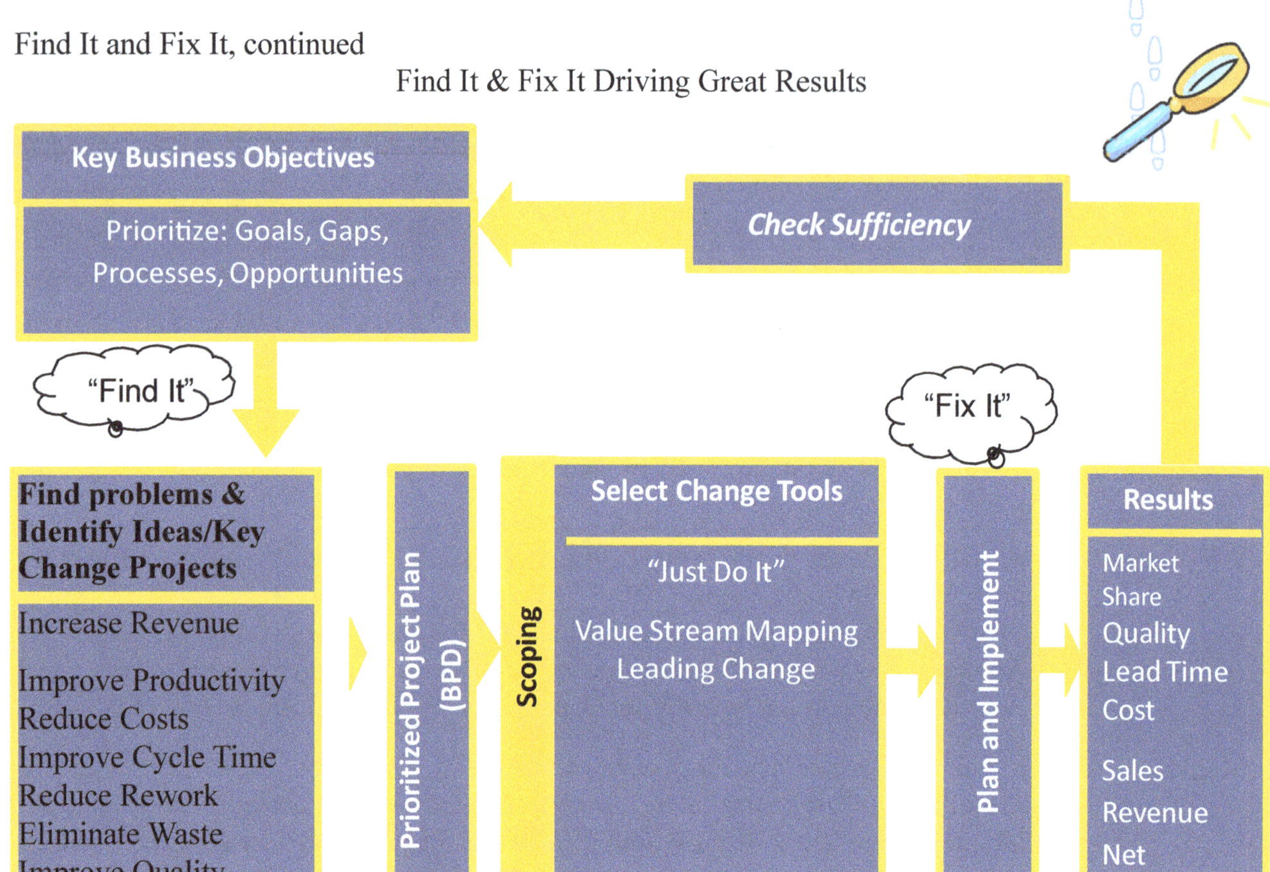

* Six Sigma, Theory of Constraints, Red X, etc.

Tips:
1. Customer expectations must never be compromised in any improvement process. Ensure your customer expectations are well- understood.
2. Understand where business objective resources are utilized/spent in your business by breaking down larger work streams into smaller processes. Identify the value or relative proportion of the business objective for each identified process within each work stream. Then, work on improving the high-resource areas first.
3. To help spark ideas in advance of an idea-generation for improvement meeting:
   - Provide the Functional Leaders with the identified Work Streams and associated Processes along with the corresponding business objective values
4. Hold a meeting to Solicit ideas/improvement opportunities from all employees involved in the processes. Use an "Idea Generation Worksheet" to get creativity flowing (see example on next page).
5. Make sure the projects you select support business objectives/goals.
6. Utilize "Business Plan Deployment" (BPD) to prioritize the selected ideas the organization will pursue to achieve business results. The ideas will become the BPD objectives and once scoping is completed, the "tools used" will become the BPD methods.
   e.g. Ensure there is a strong implementation plan at the end of each project with owners and due dates clearly understood. Schedule a regular review with owners and leadership to ensure completion.
   Ensure the discipline to "check results" is a part of the standardized work of leadership.

Idea Generation Worksheet

| Idea to Improve Business Results | Major Work Stream | Check One | | | Cross Functional Impact Y or N | Degree of Difficulty to Implement H, M, or L | Impact on Business Target H, M, or L | Structural Cost Impact Est. $ | Natural Owner (One Name Only) |
		Stop ☐	Do Less ☐	Improve ☐					

Business Plan Deployment (BPD)

What is it? **Business Plan Deployment (BPD)** is a process that enables the total organization to set targets, integrate plans, and remain focused to achieve company-wide goals and manage change.

Why use it? To create a Common Process that:
- Provides focus and direction to the organization
- Establishes clear and quantifiable targets
- Visually communicates to everyone
- Identifies opportunities for improvements (drives Continuous Improvement)
- Aligns business activities focused on objectives
- Tracks performance
- Engages/Empowers the workforce to affect Business Performance

Steps:
1. A business organization must first develop
   - a good corporate VISION
   - a MISSION statement from the functional area
2. To support the vision and mission, realistic/concrete GOALS must be developed
3. The goals are broken down into specific OBJECTIVES
4. Clear TARGETS are defined which can measure achievement of objectives
5. METHODS are developed to reach the targets
6. All of the above is held together by formal COORDINATION, and progress determined through regular and consistent REVIEWS
7. Everything is documented on the BPD form

Tips:
1. Use the standard BPD format that includes: goals, objectives, methods, targets, responsible persons, timing, sign-off, and signature block.
2. Communicate the company goals to employees before the start of the year's planning.
3. Post the BPD in a visible location following the Plan, Do, Check, Act (PDCA) format and the five goal categories of Safety, People, Quality, Responsiveness, Cost (SPQRC), and indicate on the plan when activities have been completed or create action plans for all countermeasures.

BPD, continued

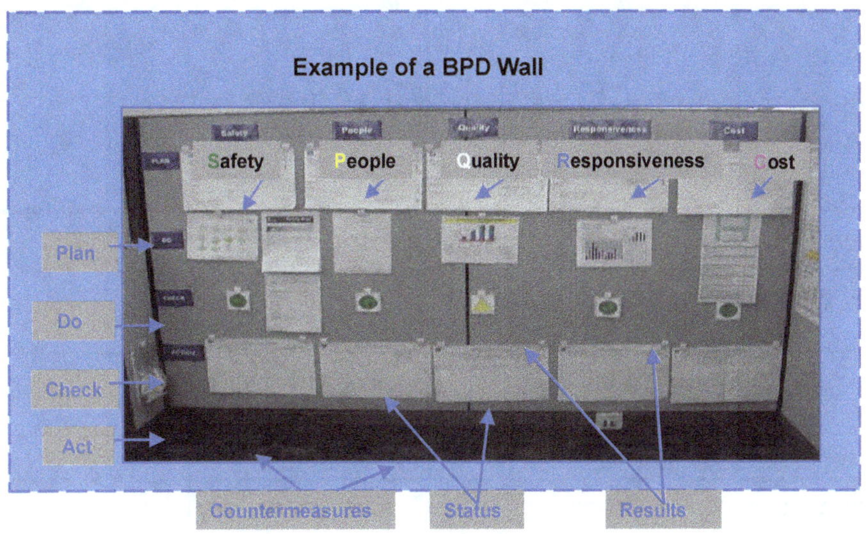

The BPD can play a key role in Visual Management.

4. Use the Plan, Do, Check, Act cycle to carry out Business Plan Deployment. Following this common process will aid in understanding and make it a more useful process.
5. Establish, standardize, and communicate an annual planning cycle (e.g. completion dates for planning, etc.) that adheres to a timeline. This will ensure enough time is allowed for thorough planning.
6. Use a formal process of negotiation and cross-functional inter-departmental meetings and sign-off blocks to assure buy in.
7. Write additions or changes to the plan, directly on the BPD. No erasing. This will permit you to SEE and track the progress.
8. Holding scheduled reviews of the plan at all levels to evaluate the progress to the goals will keep everyone informed.
9. During reviews, add the "Status" of the Objectives and Methods to the BPD. This will aid in Visual Management.

10. Develop a Countermeasure for any objective or method that receives a Yellow or Red status. This will identify what the real problems are and what is needed to get the project back on track.
11. Ensure that all employees are knowledgeable in the basic principles of BPD to the appropriate level of detail.

Working With Ideas

15 Words

What is it? **15 Words** is used to help a group summarize and clearly articulate an issue, problem statement, project definition, or the scope of the overall change initiative. The subject can range from detailed to general.

Why use it? Group members are frequently called on to describe the initiative and having a succinct definition is important. The statement created from the 15 Word activity can help in:

1. Casual conversation with others, whether they are peers, managers, sponsors, or senior executives
2. Various communications about the initiative when there is limited to give great detail on the initiative
3. Having The entire group must be able to credibly and quickly describe what they are working on

15 Words is useful when consolidating many thoughts or ideas into one concise statement. This tool can be used at various points in a meeting when information needs to be consolidated and consensus needs to be reached. Some typical uses include:

1. In the scoping process to define the "issue" to be addressed
2. During the meeting to define a single problem statement from a group of post-it notes or a list of possible issues; this is true for each recommendation problem statement
3. Various communications such as invitation notes and kick-off messages to explain what the group is going to work on
4. This process also works for developing mission statements

Steps:

1. After some initial discussion by the group, have each group member (or in pairs or small groups) write their definition of the project/issue/problem in 15 words or less on post-it notes, a flip chart, or a blank overhead transparency
2. Share the outcomes with the full group (for example, if done on flipcharts, have group members walk around to review others' 15 words)
3. As a group, identify the key terms/themes where agreement exists and circle, underline, or highlight key words
4. Draft a working statement using the key words that capture the essence from various versions; revise with the group to reach an agreed upon definition and test for consensus
5. Either reach a consensus on the 15 word description as a group, or ask someone to continue to refine it and present later to the group for review

Tips:
1. If the team/group is large (e.g., 8 or more), consider doing step 1 in pairs or small groups
2. Reviewing, integrating, and reaching consensus is more laborious and challenging the more sets of 15 Words there are; keeping the number of sets to 5 or fewer can be helpful
3. Choose the method and materials that the individuals/small groups use to note their initial 15 Words based on the size of the room and group
4. It can be more efficient and less laborious if group members can walk around and review the descriptions — hence flipcharts can be useful if the room is big enough
5. If an overhead projector is available and it is impractical to use flipchart pages, use transparencies.
6. If the leader is comfortable doing so, have him/her run steps 3 and 4
7. If not, the facilitator may do so, taking guidance from the leader
8. Generally it is easier to assign/volunteer someone to develop a 15 Word description outside the group; however, if the group appears close to a consensus, do it with the full group
9. If the statement is revised outside the group, make sure a formal review is done by the entire group

---

Instructions:

1. Have each group member or small group write in 15 words or less the definition of the project, issue or problem statement using either large post-it notes, a flip chart page, or an overhead transparency
2. Review each statement with the total group
3. As a group, identify the key terms/themes where agreement exists; circle the key words or phrases
4. Highlight and clarify all unclear words by asking "What do you mean by this?"
5. Draft a working statement using the key words from each person or group; after the statement has been crafted, test for consensus and agree on a statement
6. It is also permitted to agree on a working version that can be fine tuned or rewritten later

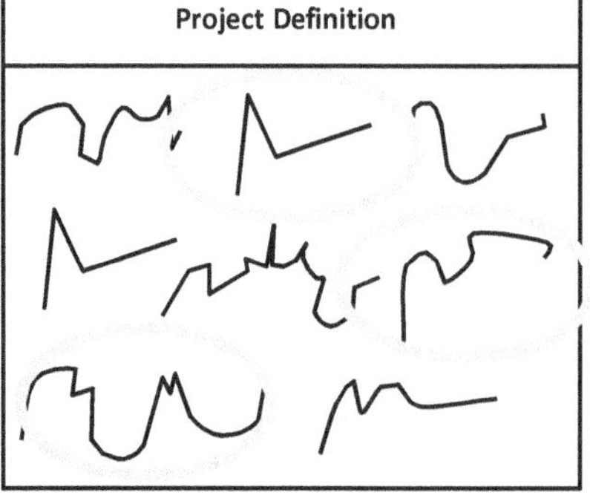

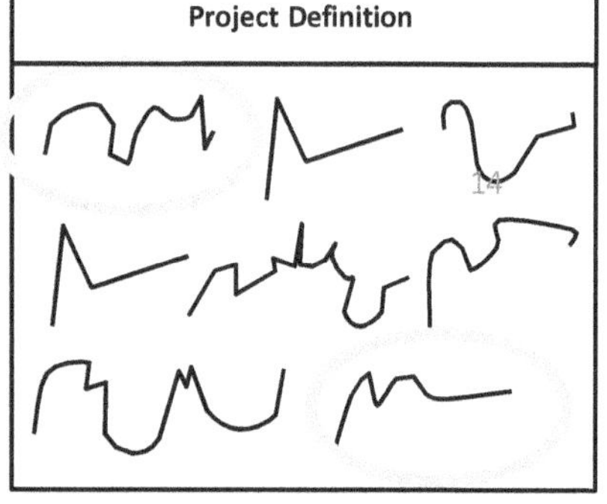

Backward Imaging

What is it? **Backward Imaging** is a way for group members to imagine what success with the initiative will look like in behavioral terms and what it will take to get there.

Why use it? It is a succinct means of having the group:
1. Describe the visible impact of successfully implementing a solution to the issue(s) of their initiative
2. Identify and communicate what needs to be different in order to solve the issue (i.e., what key stakeholders/constituents will be doing differently)
3. Begin to identify which behaviors need to be changed and how they can be changed in order to reach a successfully implemented solution
4. Uncover unanticipated support or resistance

Steps: Set up the group individually or in pairs/small groups to:
1. Imagine a point in the future when the initiative has been implemented and is very successful
2. Describe what you would see, as you observe the key players functioning in the new, improved state
3. Identify changes, critical actions, and decisions that it took to successfully implement the changes, as well as identify
key results obtained, "sacred cows" addressed, etc.

As a total group, discuss and capture the key points group members had:
1. Discuss the key actions/changes needed to get to a successful implementation of a solution
2. Press for what will be different between this initiative and the typical initiative at the unit involved; often there is insufficient thought about how to engage the right people in implementing the solution
3. Reach conclusions about the group's goals/desired results, if they have not yet been defined
4. Summarize the key takeaways that have implications for the group's work and action plans

Tips: This exercise can be set up as if the group were writing an article in a well-regarded business journal (e.g., in the U.S., *Fortune* or *Harvard Business Review*). Group members, either individually or in pairs, can then:

1. Note how indicate what this stands for (COE) (or the head of the unit) describes to the author the before and after of the issue the group is addressing
2. Describe what key stakeholders said during interviews with the reporter about what changed and how the changes occurred to cause the issue to be addressed
3. Ask why this change initiative was so much more successful than previous attempts
4. Continue describing what the author and those he/she interviewed saw and how key constituents were operating in the improved state
5. Create an interesting title for the story

Brainstorming

What is it?   **Brainstorming** is a tool that is used for collecting information on a given topic. It is typically used to collect group input in a quick manner.

Why use it?   Brainstorming creates a framework for all members to share their ideas and to generate a list of items for further discussion. The listed information can be utilized in problem solving, decision-making, and/or action planning. Brainstorming is meant to be an engaging, creative process for groups to gather and capture their ideas on a wide-range of subjects. It can serve as an easy way to engage a group in a discussion.

Steps:

1. Clearly state the topic to be discussed
2. Cover the ground rules for brainstorming listed on the next page
3. Write information on a flip chart or whiteboard to make ideas visible
4. Record <u>every</u> idea
5. Build on ideas already stated – piggyback, connect new ideas to existing ideas
6. Hear everyone's ideas
7. Defer discussion, judging, or questioning
8. After list is complete, discuss items, prioritize, combine, and ask clarifying questions

Other Variations
1. Participants work individually first by writing down their ideas
2. Everyone records ideas on large post-it notes that are posted
3. Use a roundtable approach to ask for ideas by rotating from table to table or person to person
4. Subgroups rotate from topic to topic, recording ideas
5. Rotate subgroups from topic to topic, recording ideas on a flip chart

Brainstorming Guidelines

<table>
<tr><td>Describe topic…</td></tr>
<tr><td>

- *Generate as many ideas as possible*
- *Do not evaluate ideas: no idea is a bad idea*
- *Give everyone an opportunity to share his or her ideas*
- *Build on ideas to create additional ideas*
- *Capture all ideas that are expressed*
- *Keep going for as long as possible*
- *Reassure everyone that all of their ideas are equal*
- *Ask clarifying questions*

</td></tr>
</table>

Circles of Control, Influence, Concern

What is it?   **Circles of Control, Influence and Concern** (CCIC)is a framework for groups to use to sort information. The goal is to use this tool to identify what the group has control and influence over so they spend their time working on things they can truly impact.

Why use it?   The power of this tool is to focus the group in areas that they can impact. It is the a "visual" that can facilitate great discussions. CCIC It is especially useful when a group member or members are stuck on a topic that is out-of-scope. This tool may help name this situation and allows the group to move on to more fruitful discussions. If the subject is critical and becomes a roadblock to progress, yet it is not within the group's circle of control or influence, a group may need to involve others to address the issue.

Steps:
1. Draw circles on a chart and post for easy reference
2. Present the model as a framework for determining what to work on
3. Explain that the CCIC is based on Stephen Covey's work about effective people spending the majority of their energy
   working on things within their control or influence
4. If using this tool to sort ideas, have the group members place ideas in the appropriate circles
5. If using it to brainstorm things to work on, have the group members generate topics and then place the ideas in the appropriate circles
6. For important issues that fall in the concern ring, identify the stakeholders to involve and plan how to influence them
7. Encourage the group to be realistic in assessing what they have control over, yet not be too conservative
8. Move to problem solving or action planning, focusing on the items in the inner circles

Tips:

1. Always have the chart posted so it can be referenced when the group goes off track
2. When many items fall in the "concern" ring, ask the group if the leader needs to be involved to reframe their task, or if other people who have control or influence need to be engaged
3. For key items that fall in the "concern" ring, ask if some aspects of it can be within their control or influence – get specifics
4. Use this chart as a parking lot for issues that fall out-of-scope for this session
5. Can be used before the workshop with the leader in identifying appropriate participants and decision panel members
6. Can also be used to remind people before brainstorming or problem solving to focus on areas within their circles of control and influence
7. Use as a check point for recommendations – is this something within our control? Can we influence the stakeholders to support our recommendation?
8. Use as a point of clarification at a gallery prior to people "dot voting" on topics to work on (see Dot Voting tool)

Circles of Control, Influence, Concern Tool

Instructions:

1. Explain the three rings of the model, explain most productive work falls into the inner two rings
2. Agree on what our group has control, influence, or just concern
3. Post information on the chart in the appropriate area
4. Discuss the "concern" and "influence" aspects, identify key stakeholders you should involve and plan how to increase your control or to exercise your influence

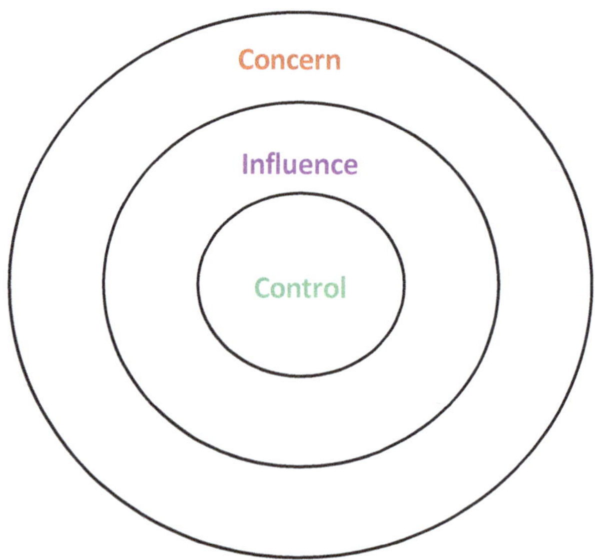

Diagnostic Questions and *Leading Change* Profile

What is it?   The **Diagnostic Questions and *Leading Change* Profile** — designed to be used together — are meant to measure the organization's or a business unit's change implementation capability, to track changes, and to generate discussion of the specific implementation challenges. Through debate and discussion, the group develops a profile of the seven success factors related to their specific change initiative.

Why use it?   The tool's initial application can be useful to:
1. Assess the overall change implementation capability of the organization or business unit
2. Identify the organization's change implementation strengths that can be leveraged for change initiatives
3. Identify the organization's change implementation improvement opportunities and begin to determine areas to work on
4. Develop an initial baseline for the group's action planning

For many groups, this is an eye-opening exercise which helps them chart a new course for the change initiative they are working on. At a minimum, the tool provides the group with an opportunity to confront and deal with the current change situation. The on-going application of the tool can be used to:
1. Assess what areas the group should focus on improving
2. Determine how to make those improvements
3. Track changes in the group's change capabilities throughout an initiative

Steps: 1. Review Leading Change model to explain the 7 success factors
2. Have each group member answer the diagnostic questions for each of the seven success factors to come up with a rating for each
3. Have group members post their scores on a profile chart (using dots works well)
4. Summarize the group's ratings for each success factor, working with the group to reach general agreement on a rating
for each factor
5. For the initial assessment and on-going group milestone assessments, discuss the answers to the Diagnostic Profile questions:
   a) What are our strengths? How do we leverage them?
   b) What are our deficiencies? How do we eliminate/overcome them?
   c) What consistencies/inconsistencies exist across respondents? Why are the perceptions of our effectiveness different? Do we need to address these inconsistencies? How?

d) What is the single most serious threat to our success, assuming that our solution/results are accepted and implemented? Who needs to address this threat, when, how?

Tips:

1. Although the initial assessment is typically done during a meeting, subsequent group assessments can be done in between meetings to allow analysis to be done prior to a meeting
2. It can be useful to keep the group's self-assessment posted at group meetings as a reminder of what it has to improve in both developing and carrying out action steps
3. As the group builds its action plan and carries out its work, it can refer to the Diagnostic Questions and Profile a to see whether it is covering the important elements to the change implementation
4. Set goals of 3.5 or above for each success factor to assure project success

The *Leading Change* Model – 7 Success Factors

Leading Change (Change Champions)
Having "champions" who create the environment for accelerated change by understanding their role, spending the time required, accepting the accountability, allocating the resources and advocating the change

Creating A Shared Need

The compelling business reason — for the organization and for individuals — to change, is instilled within the organization and widely shared; the level of need for change must exceed the level of resistance

Defining What To Do

Desired outcomes are defined and communicated; key actions to achieve outcomes are clearly understood; measurable targets are set

Mobilizing Stakeholders

Key stakeholders and sources of potential resistance are identified and a practical plan to overcome their resistance is in place; there is strong commitment from key constituents

Acting On Decisions

The key decisions, and who is accountable for making them, have been identified; the resources required to support a realistic action plan have been secured

Monitoring, Learning, Adapting

Progress is visible; measurable indicators guarantee accountability, plans are revised based on feedback; learning is made specific and applied widely

Changing How We Manage
Making sure that management processes, including rewards, measures, communication, structure, capability building, technology, and resource allocation, reinforce both the action plans and the environment for change

---

5 = **Exceptional:** We have this completely taken care of
4 = **Good**: We are in fine shape; this is not a concern
3 = **Fair:** We have made progress, but this remains a concern
2 = **Problematic:** We have not addressed this or have not yet been successful in our efforts
1 = **Roadblock:** This is a problem; it could derail us

Diagnostic Questions Tool

7 Success Factors	Diagnostic Questions	Score (1-5)
Leading Change Engaging leaders who provide resources, remove obstacles, and take accountability for success	1. Is there clear ownership and a mandate for change from leaders? 2. Do all leaders understand their roles and the actions they must take? 3. Do leaders pass the "calendar test" (devote enough time)? 4. Are leaders fluent in the issues, problems, and solutions? 5. Are leaders accountable and willing to hold others accountable?	
Creating A Shared Need Establishing a compelling case for change	1. Have we gathered/created data that demonstrates the need? 2. Have we framed the need as threats/opportunities and short/long-term? 3. Have we defined the benefits/consequences of changing/not changing? 4. Is the team aligned around the need and do they feel a sense of urgency? 5. Do key stakeholders understand why this is important and why now?	
Defining What To Do Setting and communicating a clear vision, key actions, performance metrics and results	1. Is the scope thoroughly defined and agreed on by all? 2. Can we concisely, compellingly, and consistently describe the outcomes? 3. Have we established clear, measurable goals and new behaviors? 4. Do stakeholders understand how their processes and behaviors must change? 5. Do we have clear timeframes within which results will be achieved?	

Mobilizing Stakeholders Involving and informing all relevant stakeholders to obtain ownership and support	1. Have we identified all players necessary for success? 2. Do key implementers clearly understand what is in it for them? 3. Do we have a plan for leveraging support and minimizing resistance? 4. Do we have a plan for regularly communicating with key stakeholders? 5. Do we have a viable plan for removing roadblocks?	
Changing How We Manage Realigning all aspects of the organization to sustain the change and deliver results	1. Do we have the right people and capabilities to succeed and achieve results? 2. Do we have the right rewards to reinforce the change? 3. Do we have sufficient financial resources to implement successfully? 4. Do we have the right data/information and technology to succeed? 5. Has the organizational structure (roles, authority, etc.) been realigned?	
Acting On Decisions Establishing accountability for results and a sense of urgency for all activities and tasks	1. Do we have clarity around what decisions must be made? 2. Do we have clear accountability for decisions and results? 3. Do we have clear deadlines/milestones around results? 4. Does the action plan reflect a action mindset (candor, bias for action, etc.)? 5. Have we secured the resources (people, technical information) required?	
Monitoring, Learning, Adapting Applying lessons learned to improve performance and results	1. Have we identified learning from previous successes/failures? 2. Have we applied principles from our experiences to improve results? 3. Do we have timely, visible measures for tracking our progress? 4. Do we have specific milestones for measuring our progress and results? 5. Have we adjusted our strategies, action plans, and behaviors?	

Leading Change Profile Tool

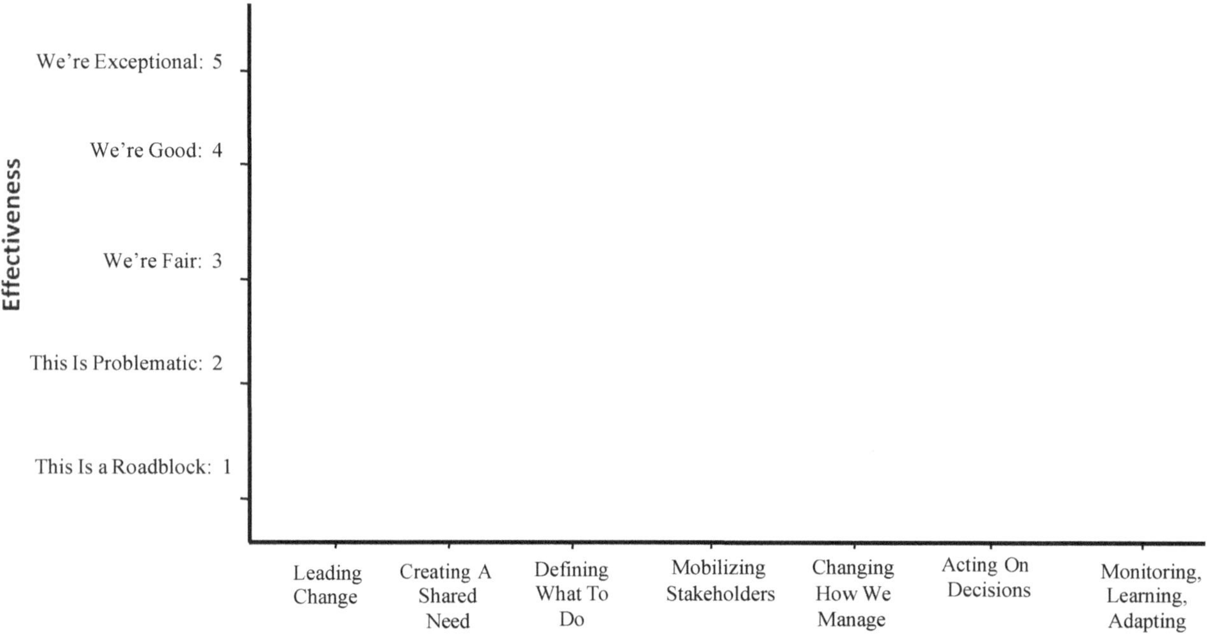

***Leading Change* Success Factors**

Dot Voting

What is it?   **Dot Voting** is a mechanism for polling the group and visually capturing the responses. It helps group members sort priorities from among several ideas or options. Often used with a Gallery of Issues to help select the most important issues for action recommendations.

Why use it?   Dot voting is used to reduce the number of items to a workable number and to select top choices from a larger list of items, i.e., Gallery of Issues. The visual display can help facilitate dialog and increase participation in group decision-making.

Steps:

1. Give everyone a limited number of colored dot stickers (two to three) – can also use marker pens
2. Using the posted list of options, instruct everyone to distribute dots among options
3. Count dots and identify which are top priorities according to votes
4. Have the group review and discuss the results for agreement on the top priorities
5. Reduce the list to items with greatest number of dots

Small Group Ranking Technique

1. Each member selects top five among the posted list of options
2. Small groups then work together to select a single list of top five choices
3. Collect, tabulate, and write choices on flip chart
4. Narrow choices to top choice

5-3-1 Dot Ranking

1. Distribute one dot sticker of each of three colors to each participant, Red is five points, Yellow is three, Blue is one
2. Post list of options
3. Ask participants to place their red sticker on the area they feel most strongly about and the other two in decreasing order of priority
4. Tabulate the scores

Tips:

1. Don't use these as hard and fast votes, rather to narrow attention and create more focused discussion
2. Push back on "why didn't this make your list?" if necessary
3. Okay to vote on individual ideas or categories – be clear when giving the directions

Dot Voting Tool

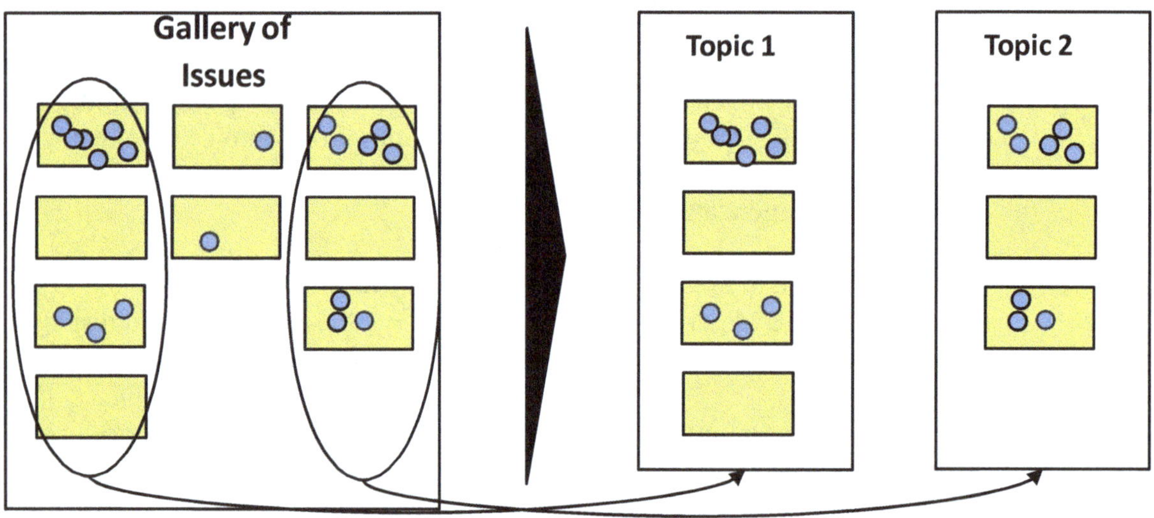

Elevator Speech

What is it?	The **Elevator Speech** is a means for the group to develop a brief description of the initiative and agree on a consistent message to be delivered to those interested in the group's work.
Why use it?	The reasons for using the Elevator Speech are that it:

1. Helps group members understand the initiative by having them describe it in their own words
2. Increases the understanding of the initiative and its potential impact on the company/unit
3. Provides group members with a consistent message for all interested parties
4. Helps develop communiqués about the group's initiative

Steps:

1. After applying at least one scoping tool and usually discussing the business reason for this work, the group would discuss the purpose of the tool
2. Either individually or in pairs/groups, ask each group member to develop a brief Elevator Speech (that can be recited in ≤60 seconds) that describes:
   a. The initiative
   b. Why the initiative is important
   c. What needs to be changed/improved
   d. What success will look like
   e. What we need from each key stakeholder
3. Have each member or pairing/grouping of members read their Elevator Speech out loud; designate a timekeeper
4. Capture the key messages in each of the five categories (done by a facilitator or the group leader to help in
developing the group's Elevator Speech)
5. Based on the group members' Elevator Speeches, the leader subsequently develops an overall Elevator Speech that is shared with the group

Tips:

1. Before developing an Elevator Speech, group members should have been through a scoping exercise
2. Consider assigning different stakeholders to individual or small group to develop targeted messages
3. Assign the Elevator Speech as homework to be completed between group meetings
4. Different group members can be assigned different roles: specific stakeholder; timer/elevator operator; critic; etc.
5. Create a consolidated group Elevator Speech should be developed based on the input from the group members

Elevator Speech Tool

<table>
<tr><td>

Instructions:

1. Imagine a chance meeting with a key stakeholder in an elevator.
2. The key stakeholder asks, "I heard you are working on the _________________________initiative. What's it all about?"
3. Prepare and practice a short answer to that question which can be delivered in 60 seconds or less.

</td></tr>
</table>

Guidelines:
Good Elevator Speeches normally contain:
- Here's what our initiative is about
- Here's why it is important
- Here's what we need to change
- Here's what success will look like
- Here's what we need from you

My elevator speech:

Fist to Five and Thumbs Up

What are they? **Fist to Five and Thumbs Up** are methods for checking consensus and reaching group decisions.

Why use them? When a group is working on solving a problem or reaching a decision, having a visual means for polling the group is very helpful. Either of these techniques gives a quick visual read on level of agreement, identifies who needs to discuss things more and who is ready to move on to a decision. Fist to Five and Thumbs Up enables the group to determine if there is agreement or disagreement among the group members and assures everyone is heard.

Steps:
1. After some amount of discussion, anyone in the group can ask to check for consensus
2. Choose one of the methods and explain how it works
   a. Fist to Five: use the # of fingers on one hand to signify level of agreement (fist – not at all up to five – total agreement
   b. Thumbs Up: use the position of your thumb to signify agreement (thumb up), unsure, need more discussion (thumb sideways), against (thumb down)
3. For group members at less than four or five or without a thumbs up, ask them to explain what remains to be discussed or resolved

Tips:
1. Make sure that the decision is appropriate for consensus and total commitment from all group members is required
2. Have someone clearly state the decision to be made or topic to be voted on
3. Continue to discuss points of difference and periodically test for progress
4. Fist to Five: Ask people to indicate how close to agreement they are by displaying the appropriate number of fingers:
   5 = fully committed
   4 = close enough to fully support it
   3 = getting there, close, need more information
   2 = still a ways to go
   1 = skeptical
   Fist = total disagreement
5. Thumbs Up: Ask people to indicate how close to agreement they are by displaying their thumbs in one of three ways:
   Thumbs Up = fully committed, total agreement
   Thumbs Sideways = unsure, want more discussion
   Thumbs Down = skeptical, disagreement, need lots more discussion
6. For participants showing less than four, ask them to state what makes them uncomfortable with the decision and what it will take to get to 4 or 5
7. Make sure everyone is participating and not showing disagreement or disengaging by abstaining

Force-Field Analysis

What is it?   **Force-Field Analysis** helps groups identify the processes, systems, and people that will support or impede the group's efforts in successfully implementing their improvements.

Why use it?   Force-Field Analysis helps groups:
1. Identify barriers to address and successfully implement their proposed changes
2. Determine what organizational factors can help the group's efforts to implement their initiative
3. Begin to determine how to change, minimize, or remove obstacles to successful implementation and integrate them into their action plans
4. Examine why the group is not making more or better progress, or why the group is not meeting its commitments, etc.

Steps:
1. Determine the specific topic to which the Force-Field Analysis is being applied to assure the statement or question that is being examined is agreed to by the group
2. Individually, in small groups, or as a full group identify factors (i.e., processes, systems, organization structures, metrics, capability, responsibilities/accountabilities, etc.) that either currently, or are likely to:
   a. Help in the successful implementation of the group's changes
   b. Hinder the successful implementation of the group's changes
3. Determine the helping factors that can be used to leverage or offset some of the hindering factors and prioritize or sequence (i.e., are there some hindering factors that are likely to be eliminated or made less of an issue if other hindering factors are addressed?) the hindering factors' impact on the group's changes
4. Identify items to include in an action plan; i.e., what work/steps need to be completed in order to address the hindrances and/or leverage the helpful factors?

Tips:
1. If group members' assertiveness varies significantly, the group will benefit from either having individuals or small groups identify the hindering and helping factors
2. Typically it is easier for people to identify hindering factors than helping factors
3. It can be useful to suggest some helping factors to get group members to think of additional one
4. Allow enough time to do a complete job on steps 2 and 3 above, since a large part of the value of this tool comes from the outputs that leads to actions and next steps

Force-Field Analysis Tool

Instructions:
1. List desired state in the middle of the chart
2. Identify factors (processes, systems, people, etc.) that will support (help) the success of the initiative
3. Identify factors (processes, systems, people, etc.) that will impede (hinder) the success of the initiative
4. Generate ideas on how to best remove or minimize the factors that will hinder the group's progress

Helping	Desired State	Hindering

Gallery of Issues

What is it? **Gallery of Issues** is a highly visual process for gathering, organizing, and evaluating information using post-it notes to record and display the ideas.

Why use it? After brainstorming issues, the gallery serves as a tool for sorting and grouping ideas together. Once this is done, the group can more easily decide where to focus their energy. The strength of the gallery tool is in the picture it provides to the group. The group can quickly see if there are common or divergent topics or be able to decide what is the priority topic among the many choices. By being interactive and visual, galleries are often a high energy step in a prioritization process.

Steps:

1. Read the Gallery of Issues question to the group
2. Distribute post-it notes and markers
3. Ask participants to record on post-it notes as many issues as they can identify which need to be addressed related to the topic (approximately 10 minutes)
4. Remind them:
   - Nothing is wrong or off limits!
   - Write one issue per post-it note
   - Frame issues as problems, not solutions or questions
   - Specific and concise
5. Post and discuss the issues (see options listed on next page)
6. Discard or add notes as the conversation develops
7. Have the group work to understand each author's thinking, and edit and organize the notes in a logical way, clustering and grouping post-it notes into categories:
   - Identify duplicates and/or related issues and group them accordingly
   - Refine and prioritize the ideas as many times as needed
8. Gain consensus on the groupings

<table>
<tr><td>Steps,
continued:</td><td>Use one of the following options to create the gallery:</td></tr>
</table>

Use one of the following options to create the gallery:

Option 1 — total group
- Have everyone put their post-it notes on the wall
- Work wall in sections
- Look for duplication from other post-it notes
- Have participants group, sort, clump the post-it notes, eventually involving everyone
- Add titles, themes, or headings to the groupings

Option 2 — by table
- Assign each table a facilitator - take a few minutes to review the post-it notes as a table group
- Clarify, merge, and clump post-it notes on a chart
- When the tables are finished, have each table present and then hang their post-it notes on wall
- Identify final clumps
- Add titles, themes, or headings to the groupings

Option 3 — table or total group
- Have someone put one post-it note on the wall
- Ask for anything related to that one from the entire group
- When the topic is finished, start the next clump (create topics as notes are revealed)
- Adjust as appropriate when clumps are finished

Option 4 — assigned topics
- Have pre-assigned topics posted on gallery wall
- Ask participants to hang post-it notes in the specific areas

Tips:

1. Vary the pace of information collection to maintain high group energy
2. In a larger group, have table groups sort and organize information before posting
3. Keep everyone engaged by having the group post information, move it into categories, label the categories, etc.
4. Once the gallery is complete, proceed to dot voting or some other form of prioritization to decide which topics to work on

Gallery of Issues Tool

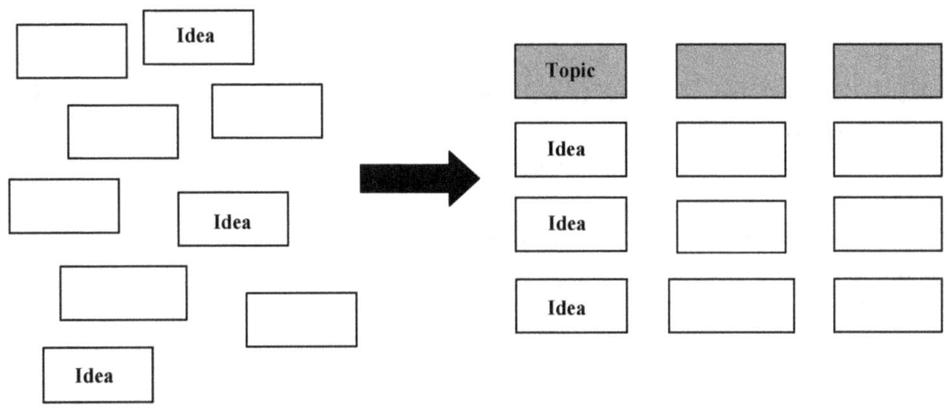

Question: What barriers and roadblocks must be addressed?

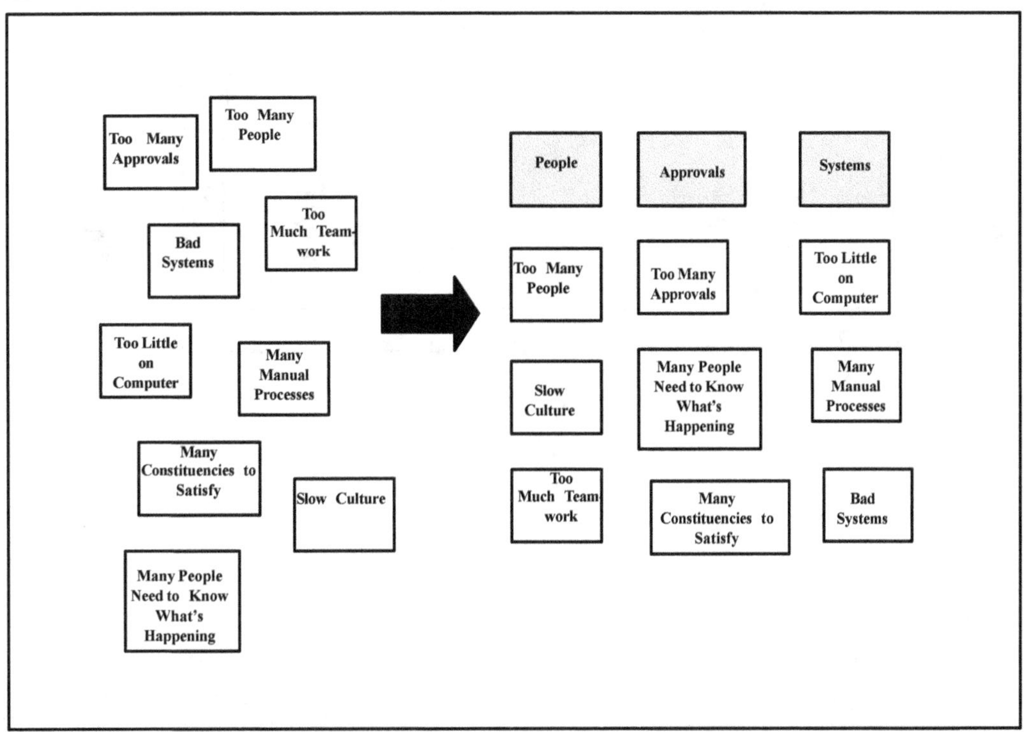

In the Frame/Out of the Frame Tool

<table>
<tr><td>

Instructions:

1. Have the leader and group list all potential aspects/components (e.g., end results, timeframe, product lines, geographic, organizations/groups involved) of the initiative using post-it notes
2. As a total group, place each idea either in-the-frame, outside-the-frame, or on-the-frame (if uncertainty or disagreement exists)
3. Discuss "on-the-frame" items in more detail to reach agreement
4. Review the group's understanding of the scope with the appropriate leaders

</td></tr>
</table>

Is/Is Not

What is it?   **Is/Is Not** helps groups consider what issues are in the group initiative's scope.

Why use it?   This tool helps groups identify the initiative's "boundaries" as well as identifying the specific issues that are within the scope of the group. It is useful because:
1. It helps clarify the scope of the initiative early in the process
2. It may shape the scope further, enabling early review by the owners of the initiative
3. It can help ensure that the appropriate resources are on the group and that some areas are not over-represented
4. It can speed the subsequent work of the group, with an early discussion and clarification of the group's scope

Steps:
1. The group describes the scope of the initiative
2. This can include a written summary, but should also include an oral description of the specific issue(s) being addressed
3. Group members brainstorm items that are and are not in scope, using post-its, or any approach that is comfortable for the group

---

Instructions:

1. Identify with the leader and the group all the things they consider in/out of scope
2. Review the ideas and identify points of disagreement
3. Establish consensus on what is in and out of scope and review this with the project owner to confirm

Is/Is Not Tool

IS	IS NOT

More of/Less of

Instructions:

1. Identify specific actions that support/reinforce the desired future state
2. Identify specific actions that impede progress towards the desired future state
3. Develop an action plan for obtaining more of the supportive behavior and less of the counter-productive behavior

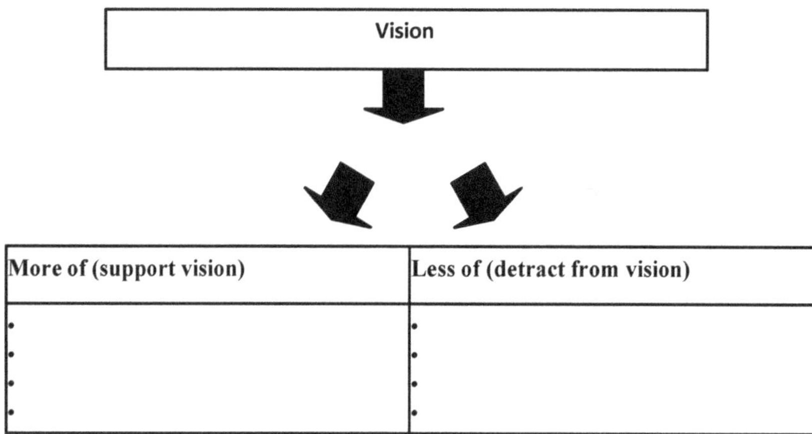

More of/Less of Tool

1. Identify specific actions that support/reinforce the desired future state
2. Identify specific actions that impede progress towards the desired future state
3. Develop an action plan for obtaining more of the supportive behavior and less of the counter-productive behavior

Tips:
1. Encourage group members individually to identify More of/Less of behaviors to prevent dominant group members from overriding less dominant group members
2. Determine the most effective means of brainstorming that will elicit all group members' views of relevant More of/Less of behaviors
3. In grouping similar behaviors, be cautious not to lose any of the noted behaviors unless group members unanimously opt to discard the behavior (i.e., the author changes his/her view)
4. Discuss actions to take to address issues

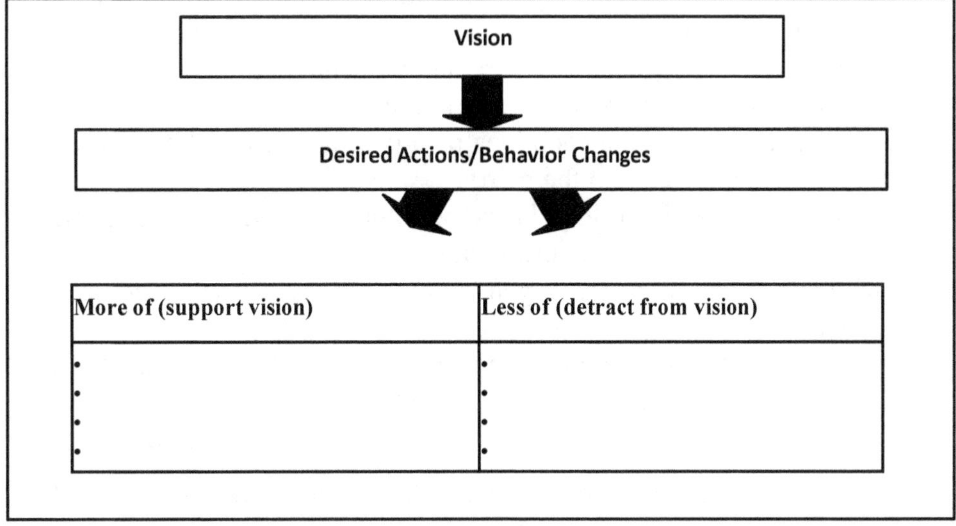

Payoff Matrix

What is it?   **Payoff Matrix** is a two-by-two table that helps sort and evaluate ideas. Typical dimensions are Payoff vs. Ease of Change; Level of Difficulty vs. Urgency; Cost vs. Benefit; Customer Impact vs. Organization Impact; Required Resources vs. Time Required to Implement; and Global vs. Local.

Why use it?   The primary reason to use a payoff matrix is to sort and prioritize actions or ideas. It serves as a discussion format to take a range of ideas and narrow down how best to spend the group's time and energy. The matrix is a visual tool that helps the group to:

1. Determine which ideas have the most benefit or require the most work related to two important dimensions
2. Discuss each idea or issue in an organized manner resulting in thoughtful discussions before beginning to problem solve
3. Begin the process of identifying where the team wants to focus their energy by sorting priorities and understanding the thinking behind other people's ideas
4. Uncover support, resistance, and areas of agreement or disagreement

Steps:
1. Select the two dimensions that best fit the discussion topic to construct the matrix
2. Decide on the words that describe the extremes (high to low, difficult to easy)
3. Draw the matrix on a flip chart to facilitate engagement and discussion
4. Draw the matrix so the most desirable box is the upper right hand corner; explain the matrix to the group before beginning to add the post-it notes
5. Brainstorm ideas and put each idea on a post-it note as a total group, discuss each post-it note and place into the matrix
6. Depending on the situation, this can be solutions to address the specific issue or on bigger topics, aspects of the problem to tackle
7. Encourage the group to identify and add any other ideas they come up with during the discussion
8. After all post-it notes are on the matrix, discuss and decide which ones to tackle to begin problem solving and action planning
9. Address each post-it note with action plans or make a decision not to resolve the item.

Tips:
1. Encourage the group to work on items that fall in the most optimum boxes
2. Actively facilitate the process so it doesn't get bogged down in debate regarding where an idea falls; if there is major disagreement, check to see if the idea can be rewritten more clearly or broken into multiple ideas
3. Encourage the group to make a decision about all the items – to resolve, eliminate, or defer so that items aren't left hanging
4. When possible, have the group stay very actively involved in this sorting process
5. If it becomes necessary to stop and problem solve an item during the sorting process, go with the group's energy and return to the matrix if necessary

Payoff Matrix Tool

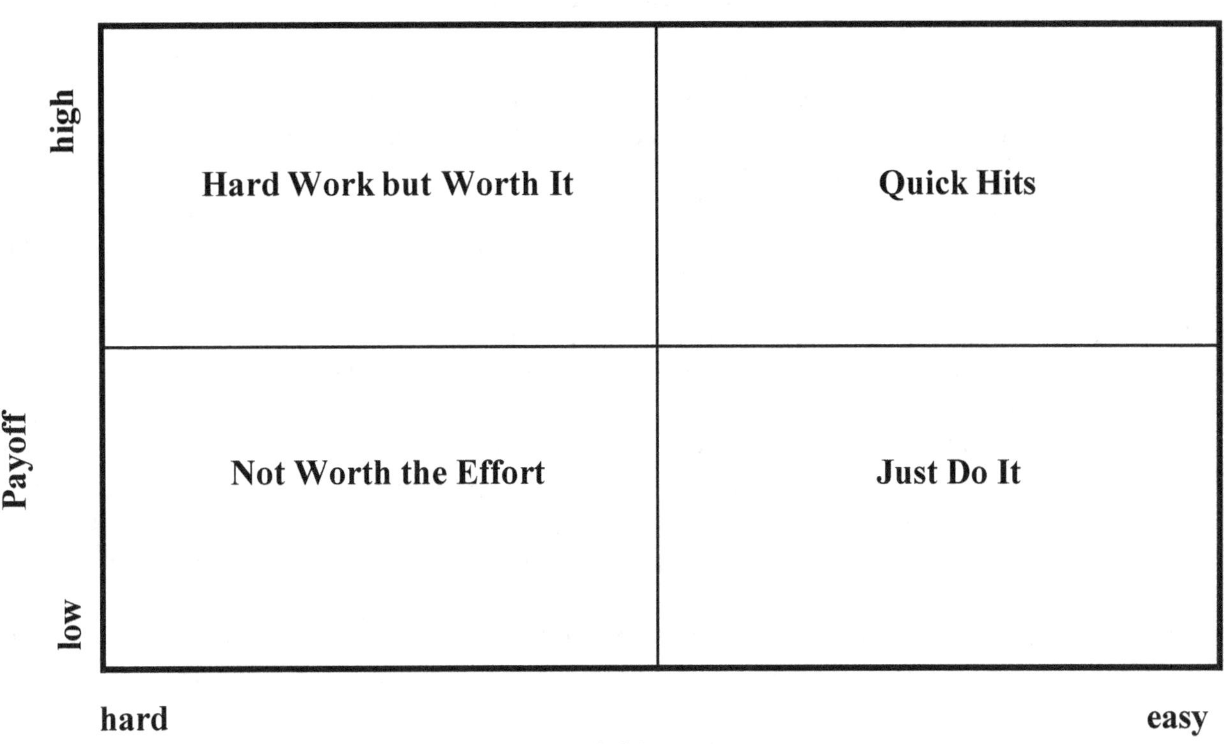

Purpose Statement

What is it?   The **Purpose Statement** is used to define the project. It consists of 2 components:
- Why we are doing the workshop? A simple statement that highlights the current issues with the process
- What we want to achieve? Expected results defined in terms of measurable metrics aligned to the business goals of Safety, People, Quality, Responsiveness, and Cost (SPQRC)

Why use it?   This tool is critical for defining the purpose and objectives of the workshop. Developing the Purpose Statement enables the stakeholders to:
1. Create a shared need that is supported by all
2. Validate that the project is important and worth the effort
3. Clearly identify goals and objectives to build momentum and energy to drive the improvement effort
4. Establish a baseline for measuring continuous improvement after implementation

Steps:
1. Solicit stakeholder input on what is wrong with the current process/situation. What doesn't work well? What are other symptoms of the problem? Capture input on a list.
2. Using the above list of issues, facilitate discussion to formulate a clear, focused statement on the purpose of the workshop and the expected outcomes.
3. Facilitate discussion to identify clear, measurable metrics to measure the performance of the current process as well as the improved process.
4. Refine and finalize the Purpose Statement through scoping, prior to the workshop.

Tips:

1. Write the proposed objectives in everyday language.
2. Include metrics to measure project success and performance of the improved process. Use phrases such as:
    - *Reduce lead-time by ... (OR) Reduce lead-time from ... to ...*
    - *Improve First Time Quality by ... (OR) Improve First Time Quality from ... to ...*
    - *Eliminate rework by x % (OR) Reduce rework from ... to ...*
    - *Minimize number of handoffs ... (OR) Reduce handoffs from ... to ...*
    - *Decrease work-in-process by ... (OR) Decrease work-in-process from ... to ...*
3. Challenge teams to identify how they can measure how well the process is working today. Have stakeholders gather data and/or estimates of current performance on these measures.
4. Try to align metrics around the business goals of SPQRC.

SIPOC

What is it?   **SIPOC** is a process-oriented tool that pieces together the major elements of a process/value stream to allow participants the ability to view it at a high-level and agree on it. The term "SIPOC" consists of the first letter of the five major pieces in a process, consisting of **S**uppliers to the process, **I**nputs provided by the suppliers, **P**rocess Steps – the main steps of the process, **O**utputs for the customer, and **C**ustomers of the process. Once every element of the SIPOC is identified, a group can easily identify the starting point and the stopping point of the process. If all the elements of the SIPOC cannot be identified, it may indicate the lack of a clearly-defined process.

Why use it? The SIPOC tool is useful because it:

1. Verifies the existence of a process
2. Helps clarify the scope of the initiative/project early in the scoping process
3. Sets clear boundaries of where the project starts and stops in terms of the overall scope of work
4. Helps a group determine the most effective level of detail that will be addressed in the project
5. May shape the scope further, enabling early review by the sponsor of the initiative/project
6. May help re-shape the group to ensure that the appropriate resources are in the group and that some areas are not over-represented
7. Provides early discussion and clarification of the group's scope which will speed up the subsequent work of the group

Steps:

1. Obtain a general description of the scope of the initiative from the leader, process owner, or subject matter expert. This should include a summary of the specific issue(s) being addressed
2. Identify the customer(s) of the process
3. Identify the outputs/final products to the customer(s)
4. Identify the high-level steps to the process (optimal is 5-10 steps)
5. Clearly identify the "start" and "stop" points of the process (start point should be prior to the first process step and stop point should be immediately after the last process step)
6. Identify the suppliers and inputs to the process
7. Document/Summarize the conclusions/output of this tool for later reference

Tips:

1. It is useful to apply this tool early in the scoping process.
2. This tool can be used with groups of participants or in a discussion with key leaders. All participants should eventually agree on the final SIPOC.
3. Work with the process owner in advance to define the SIPOC "before" the scoping meeting to save time and to avoid getting side tracked into unproductive detail.
4. Start with "identifying the customer." It is always important to agree on the customer and the expectations of the customer before identifying the other elements of the process.
5. Groups may be confused as to whether the customer is the "final customer" (the person buying the G.M. vehicle) or the "next customer" in the process. Typically, a value stream project will identify the "next customer" as the key customer, although the final product to the "final customer" can never be compromised.
6. Although it is important to identify your customer first, the remaining categories of the SIPOC can be obtained in any order. Agreeing on the information and getting it documented is more important than the order it is obtained.
7. Questions you may use to guide participants through the SIPOC are:
    a. Who are the customers of our initiative's process (i.e., units, functions, or positions)?
    b. What is it that the customers are receiving from the process (i.e., the outputs)?
    c. What is the first step in the process? What is the final step in the process before the customer receives their product? Can you list the steps in between?
    d. Have we identified the correct start and end points for the process steps?
    e. What inputs are needed to be able to work the processes/steps that generate the outputs that the process's customer receives?
    f. Who supplies those inputs (i.e., units, functions, or positions)?
8. If participants cannot identify all the elements of the SIPOC, there is probably not a clearly identified process to improve.
9. The SIPOC provides the key steps for data gathering.

SIPOC Tool

Instructions:

1. Set up the SIPOC to include the five categories of Suppliers, Inputs, Process Steps, Outputs, and Customers of the current process
2. Identify the customer(s) of the process
3. Identify the outputs/products the customer expects
4. List the high-level steps from left to right (5-10 steps are optimal)
5. Ensure everyone agrees on the starting point and stopping point of the process
   - This will help bound what is in/out of scope of the group's work
6. Identify suppliers and inputs to the process.
7. Document the SIPOC for later use. Use the output from this exercise as a basis for project planning (stakeholder analysis, communications plan, etc.).

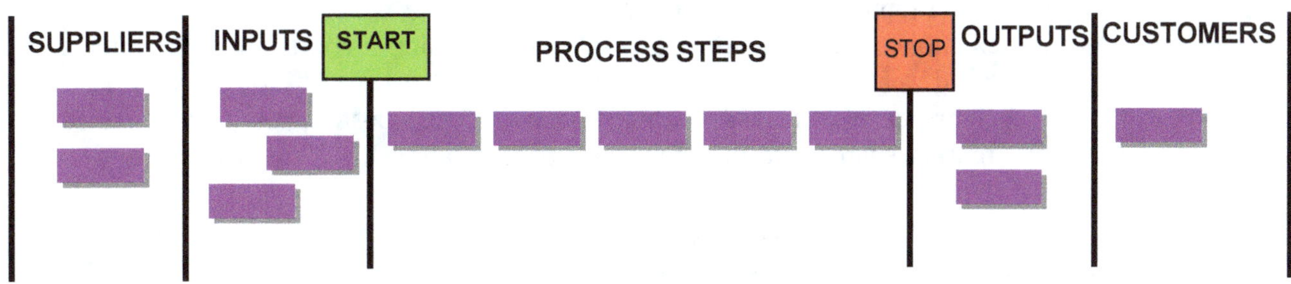

SUPPLIERS
INPUTS
START
PROCESS STEPS
STOP
OUTPUTS
CUSTOMERS

Threats versus Opportunities

What is it? **Threats and Opportunities** is designed to help the group create a "case for change."

Why use it?
1. Developing a compelling, credible case for change helps:
   a. Build enthusiasm for the initiative, both inside and outside of the immediate group
   b. Communicate the reasons for the initiative
   c. Begin to build engagement to successfully implement an initiative
   d. Identify possible metrics for the group's initiative
2. The tool helps the group develop key, succinct messages regarding the initiatives and expected outcomes

Steps:
1. Identify the internal and external factors that represent short- and long-term threats for topic being addressed by the initiative
2. For example, in a prevention of quality problems initiative, some of the threats identified were:
   - Short-term: increased warranty costs, reduced customer loyalty, reduced market share, deterioration of supplier relationships, employee retention issues, missing objectives
   - Long-term: financial impact, decreasing brand loyalty, ultimate survival
3. Identify internal and external factors that represent short- and long-term opportunities for the topic being addressed by the initiative
4. For example, in a prevention of quality problems initiative, some of the opportunities identified were:
   - Short-term: pride of work, motivation to reduce warranty costs, desire to increase customer loyalty and market share, desire to be a proud employee
   - Long-term: new export opportunities, customers' desire to buy high-quality products, desire to build brand equity
5. Circle the key items to be reviewed and included in an action plan

Tips:
1. In discussing the threat/opportunity change drivers, consider:
   a. Examples of changes resulting from impending *threats*, and what the consequences were; these examples can be tied to the initiative or not (they can even be personal)
   b. Often compromises or less-than-optimal decisions are made when people are acting because of a threat
   c. Examples of changes resulting from perceived *opportunities* and their consequences
2. Before applying the tool, discuss with the group leader(s) some examples of change efforts in organization that are considered to be:

a. Best practice change examples
  - What drove the change?
  - What did leaders do to encourage the change?
  - What were the consequences?
b. Less-than-desired results examples
  - What drove the change?

3. Be sure to have the group get specific about how they can use the outputs of this tool in their work

Threats versus Opportunities Tool

Instructions:

1. Identify drivers (external and internal factors) that build the case for the change/initiative
2. Discuss the questions provided to begin identifying how to most effectively frame the need for this change (so that people can hear it)
3. Use this information as input to frame/customize your communications to different stakeholders based on *their* perceptions about relevant threats and/or opportunities

A. Which quadrant on the matrix does our organization/unit usually use as the reason to change?

____
____
____
______

B. Which quadrant best describes/fits how our initiative/project is viewed right now?

____
____
____
______

C. Which quadrant would be most beneficial to implementing our initiative/project? Why?

____
____
____
______

D. Which quadrant represents "best practice" in our organization; in other successful organizations?

____
____
____
______

E. Do we need to change the way our initiative/project is viewed? If so, what actions need to be taken?

____
____
____
______

Time Frame

Short Term

Long Term

	1	3
	2	4

Threat   Opportunity

Working With Problems/Waste

When you need to:	See this tool:	Page:
Eliminate waste and establish visual control of a physical environment	5 Step (5S)	45
Identify and explore the root cause of an issue or problem	5 Why Problem Solving	49
Uncover opportunities to remove waste from a process	COMMWIP	52
Identify and explore, in detail, all possible causes of a problem	Fishbone	57
Identify the most important and frequent problems to work on first	Pareto Principle	59

5 Step

What is it? **5 Step or 5S** is used to help visualize and eliminate waste. It is used in both manufacturing and office settings by a team to create a lean environment by organizing and standardizing the workplace.

Why use it? 5S supports creation of a lean environment by organizing the workplace. 5 S is an enabler for safety, quality, cost- reduction, continuous improvement, and standardization. Once workplace organization is achieved, additional Global Manufacturing System tools can be introduced to further eliminate waste, add value to the customer, and continuously improve the workplace & business processes.

Steps:
1. Clear
2. Organize
3. Clean
4. Standardize
5. Continuous Improvement

5 Step, continued

<table>
<tr><td>Steps,
continued:</td><td>Clear</td></tr>
</table>

- Define the purpose of the area (A clear, detailed and focused statement describing the intended use of the area or process)
    - Define your areas and activities
    - Complete a purpose statement using the identified activities for each area

---

<u>Printer-Copier-Fax - Supply Room</u> *Example*
- To provide usable facilities to fax, copy and print. To provide binding capability. To provide one common area for all necessary general office supplies

---

- Red tag the area
    - Red tag items in the area *<u>that are not necessary</u>* to fulfill the purpose
        - Identify items necessary to fulfill this purpose which are not currently here
        - Complete a "to do" list for disposal or salvage of retagged items and for items needed to fulfill the area purpose
        - Take retagged items to a pre-determined marshaling area

5S To Do List

ITEM	RESPONSIBILITY	DUE DATE	COMPLETION DATE
Dispose of Red Tagged Items			

5 Step, continued

**Steps,
continued:** **Organize and Clean**
- Visually inspect the entire area:
  - Why are items located where they are?
  - Where should each item be?
  - How can wastes like motion, material movement, inventory be eliminated?
- Organize / clean as you go:
  - Are tools, supplies, and equipment easy to see, reach and return?
  - Are frequently used items easy to reach?
  - Does the area have an orderly appearance?
  - Clean the area including tools, supplies, equipment and note required repairs

- Easy to *see*, easy to *get*, easy to *return*.

**Steps,
continued:** **Standardize**
- Establish acceptable guidelines for:
  - Items out-of-place, not meeting requirements or unsafe
  - Visual Controls to maintain organization and identify out-of-standard conditions
  - **Rules of thumb**:
    - Clearly identify location of items
    - Tape around items used by more than one person
    - Tape or shadow items to improve visual management
    - Ensure ability to locate items in 30 seconds or less
    - Store commonly used tools and items openly
    - Label drawer contents

5 Step, continued

Steps,	**Continuous Improvement**
continued:	• Develop area maintenance tasks and standard layout
	• Develop inspection plan including responsibilities

Step Five – CONTINUOUS IMPROVEMENT

Example Area Layout Maintenance Form

• Maintenance Items:
  – Workplace Organization in accordance with the diagram?
  – Equipment, tools and supplies in their proper locations?
  – Tools and equipment operative?
  – Correct parts in closed storage?
  – Correct parts in containers?
  – Inventory levels appropriate?
  – Clean or dirty?

Step Five – CONTINUOUS IMPROVEMENT

Maintenance Card

Area ____

Maintenance Performed by ____________________________________ Ext ________

Maintenance Verified by ______________________________________ Ext ________

Date	Performed	Verified	Date	Performed	Verified	Date	Performed	Verified

Tips:

1. Take a "before" and "after" photographs of the area for leadership reviews
2. Defining the purpose of the area is critical to success of the 5S activity
3. Use the "Brainstorming" or "15 Word" tools to develop the area purpose statement
4. CLEAR, ORGANIZE and CLEAN steps should always support the area purpose
5. Establish a marshaling area prior to the 5S event for temporary (2 week) storage of retagged items
6. If an item has not used in the past year, strong consideration should be given to removal from the area
7. Sustain, Sustain, Sustain. Discipline is key!

5 Why Problem Solving

What is it?   **5 Why Problem Solving** is a structured process that identifies, analyzes, and eliminates the discrepancy between the current situation and an existing standard or expectation, and prevents recurrence of the root cause.

Why use it?   The purpose of the 5 Why Problem Solving process is to identify the root cause and implement countermeasures that prevent recurrence of the problem. The process provides a simple and standard approach to solving all types of problems. Its use creates a culture in which everyone is a strong problem solver promoting continuous improvement.

Steps:
1. Problem Description – Develop a general problem description. Define the problem more specifically and break it into smaller more specific problems when necessary
2. Problem Definition – Clearly define the deviation between the expected and actual results
3. Short-term Containment – Establish containment actions
4. Locating Point of Cause –Track the problem back to the location where it occurred
5. Cause and Effect Analysis – Filter through the information to find a Root Cause
6. Long-term Countermeasures – Develop countermeasures to resolve the Root Cause of the problem
7. Follow-up – Confirm the countermeasure is working, then standardize the process or method

By including these simple, standard elements in the Problem Solving process, we will be able to successfully determine the root cause of any problem and prevent it from happening in the future.

Tips:

1. Make sure that the causes are not symptoms
2. Start with likely causes and then ask which are the most likely causes before drilling down with 5 Whys
3. Depending on the problem, it can take fewer than 5 "whys" or more "whys" as necessary
4. You may uncover multiple areas for questioning, if you complete one area using "why" questioning until it is exhausted and then move onto the next
5. Plan, Do, Check, Action (PDCA) is naturally applied to the 5 Why Problem Solving Process:
   - *Plan*: encompasses grasping the situation, identifying the root cause, setting a target, and planning the countermeasure
   - *Do*: encompasses communication of the plan and the implementation of countermeasures. Monitor results and adjust as needed
   - *Check*: is the follow-up on the implemented countermeasures to check the effectiveness

- *Action*: occurs when we either standardize the countermeasures, or take action to begin the problem solving process again.

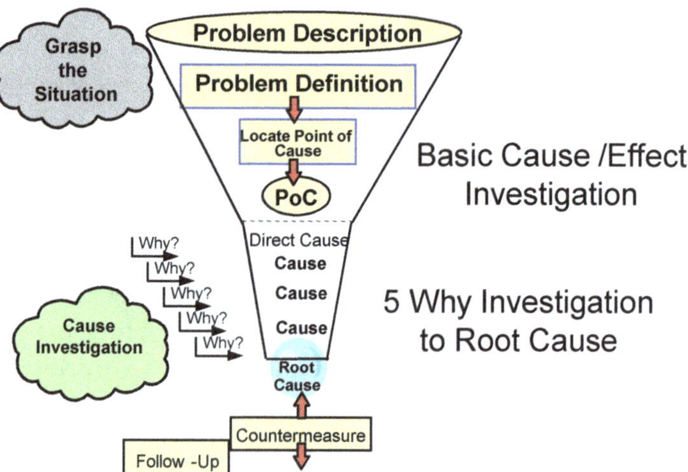

5 Why Problem Solving Tool

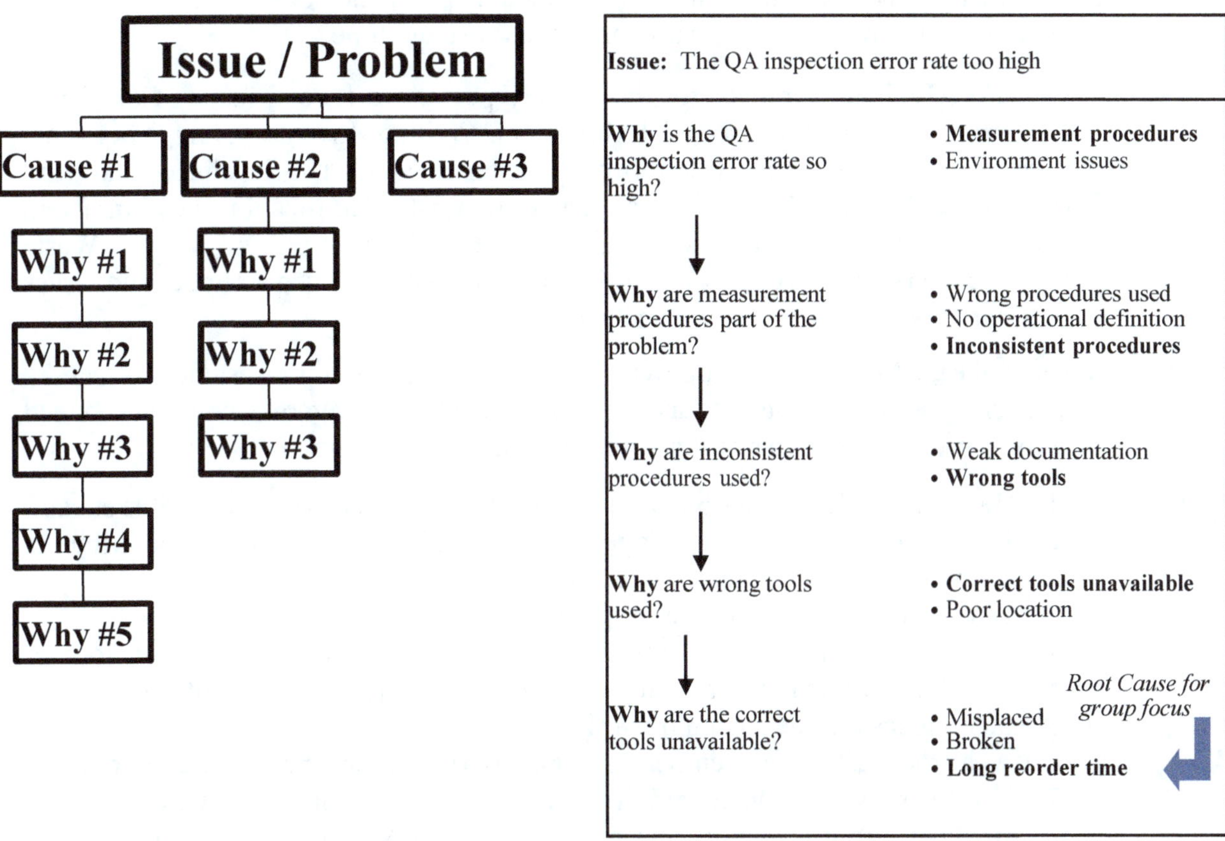

COMMWIP

What is it? **Definition of Waste:** Any element of production, processing or distribution that adds no value to the final product; waste only adds cost and time.

COMMWIP is an acronym for the seven types of waste, or Muda – **C**orrection, **O**verproduction, **M**otion, **M**aterial Movement, **W**aiting, **I**nventory, and **P**rocessing. Two main contributors to these forms of waste are Mura (Un- levelness) and Muri (Unreasonableness). COMMWIP is used during waste identification and elimination activities to focus on specific, tangible, observable examples of waste. Waste identification uncovers opportunities to remove non-value added activities and serves as a starting point for root cause analysis.

Why use it? Using the COMMWIP model provides a structured approach to waste identification, analysis, and discussion. It uncovers opportunities to remove non-value added activities and serves as a starting point for root cause analysis.

Steps:
1. Begin with a defined problem statement and area of focus (process/value stream)
2. Provide a definition of the 7 types of Waste (COMMWIP) and the contributors – Unlevelness and Unreasonableness
3. Discuss what some examples might look like
4. Provide Waste Identification template/checklist (see last page in this section)
5. Ask Observers to independently identify and document examples of waste within their process/ value stream or work area
6. As a group, ask Team members to share observations and prioritize areas of focus
7. Utilize problem solving tools (5 Why's, Fishbone Diagrams, Red X, Pareto Analysis, etc.) to identify the root causes of waste. By eliminating the root causes, the resulting waste will be eliminated.

Tips
1. Depending on the problem, not all 7 categories will be used. It is common to find multiple wastes in each task.
2. Overproduction is considered the worst waste since it contributes to all the other forms of waste.
3. Unlevelness of work flows and Unreasonable expectations of machinery and people are significant contributors to waste.
4. It is important to consider waste in the context of the value that the process provides to the ***customer.***
5. Waste is really a ***symptom*** rather than a root cause of the problem. This is why it is important to use problem solving tools to get at the root causes of waste.
6. We need to find and address ***causes*** of waste to improve flow and prevent problems from reoccurring.
7. Waste is most prevalent in the **information flow** of non-manufacturing process.

8. Conservative expert analysis suggests up to **40%** of what we do adds no value.

9. Lean thinkers look for waste **every day** in all the tasks they do and seek to eliminate it.

10. You may wish to use the "Waste Identification Checklist" at the end of this section to help employees identify waste in their work areas. The descriptions provided in the "Waste in a Business Environment" may be given to employees to remind them of the various wastes and contributors to waste to look for.

Category of Waste/Definition/Example

Waste of Correction

<u>Definition</u>: Doing something over which requires additional motion, processing, inventory and/or waiting

<u>Examples</u>: Reworking something due to error or requirement changes, reprinting informal documents to get perfect "look," starting tasks without knowing end goal, reworking a presentation/report/memo over and over again

Waste of Overproduction

<u>Definition</u>: Information too soon or too fast in a process; may cause other forms of waste

<u>Examples</u>: Unnecessary reports, too many copies, redundant work performed by different functions, preparing paper copies of documents before final version

Waste of Motion

<u>Definition</u>: Unnecessary work movements/ steps which do not add value to the product

<u>Examples</u>: Searching for misplaced items or remotely located items, holding duplicate meetings, creating non-value added steps in a process, excessive use of email and voicemail (i.e., number, length, distribution), excessive reviews, duplicate jobs

Waste of Material Movement

<u>Definition</u>: Unnecessary transporting, storing or rearranging of items, parts, equipment, people

<u>Examples</u>: Creating temporary locations for items, parts, or information and not promptly removing them when final solution is created

Waste of Waiting

<u>Definition</u>: To remain in one place while doing something other than what is related to the task at hand

<u>Examples</u>: Waiting for people, information, meetings to start on time, decisions, signature(s) for approval, sitting through the whole meeting when only a portion is relevant, unnecessary participation in meetings

Waste of Inventory

<u>Definition</u>: Too much of anything which may take up space, lead to obsolescence, impact safety, cause waste of motion or waste of material movement

<u>Examples</u>: Purchasing excessive quantity of materials, supplies, equipment, holding onto equipment in anticipation of delay in new equipment, keeping excessive supplies at desk

Waste of Processing

<u>Definition</u>: Doing something the customer does not perceive as adding value to the product

<u>Examples</u>: Complex processing of product, overly complex purchasing process, requiring redundant approvals, performing unnecessary operation or repair, performing redundant activities, typing when handwritten is sufficient, unnecessary formatting, needless reporting to multiple parties, unnecessarily carbon copying

Waste in a Business Environment
7 Types of Waste and 2 Main Contributors

Correction: Rework, work done because of errors in the previous process

Overproduction: Making more than is necessary or making things faster than is necessary, working ahead; the worst form of waste since it causes all other types of waste

Motion: Unnecessary people motions, travel, walking, searching

Material **M**ovement: Unnecessary handoffs, transfers, filing, distances of material & information

Waiting: People waiting for machines, information or people. Information waiting on people or machines

Inventory: Information or material waiting in queue

Processing: Redundant or unnecessary mental or physical work; work that is giving the customer more than he/she is willing to pay for

UnL**evelness (Mura):** A flow of information or product processes that are not regular or constant causing many of the other types of waste; the lack of consistency in schedules, products, and info.

UnR**easonableness (Muri):** Pushing a machine or people beyond their capabilities or what is considered reasonable; overburden

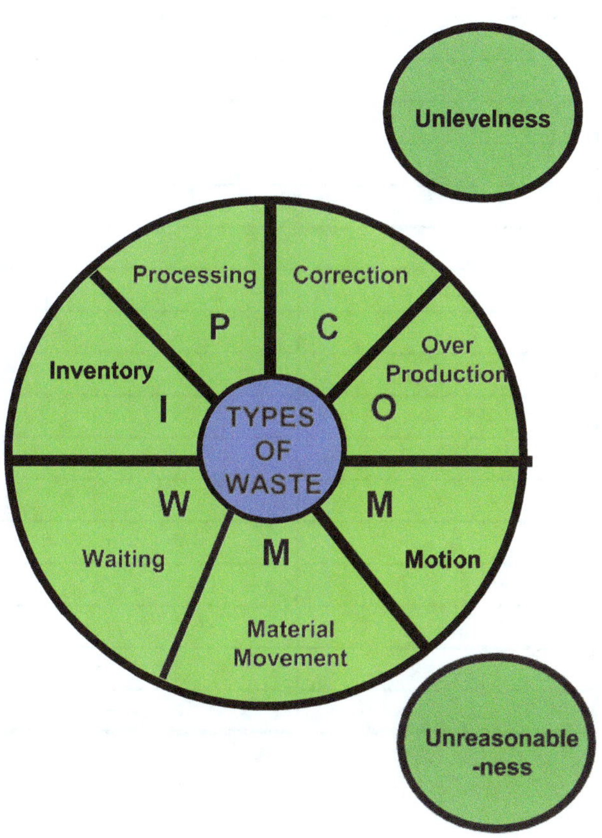

Waste Identification Checklist

#	Example	Type of Waste	Comments

7 forms of waste

1. Correction 2. Over-production 3. Motion 4. Material Movement 5. Waiting 6. Inventory 7. Processing

Fishbone

What is it? **Fishbone** helps a group analyze causes of an issue or problem in a systematic way.

Why use it? When group members are asked to determine the various causes for the problem/issue and recommend solutions with action plans to address them, this tool is useful for detailing logical connections contributing to the larger problem/issue. It can also help the group prioritize the most likely causes and identify root causes. It categorizes and provides an open systems framework for discussing the problem.

Steps:
1. Build the fishbone diagram on the wall using masking tape or draw on flip charts
2. Clarify and validate the problem with the group
3. Ask group members to identify things that are causing this problem through small group discussion or working in pairs
4. Collect their input and display the individual causes on the fishbone
5. Ask group members to cluster causes in "related clusters"
6. Test for a logical connection with the problem and label each cluster
7. Select one cluster at a time to focus on for the next step of solution generation to eliminate these causes

Tips:
1. Make sure that the causes are not symptoms
2. Take time to agree on the "head of the fish," the key issue
3. Ask "why" five times to get to the root cause
4. Combine storyboarding with this tool

Fishbone Tool

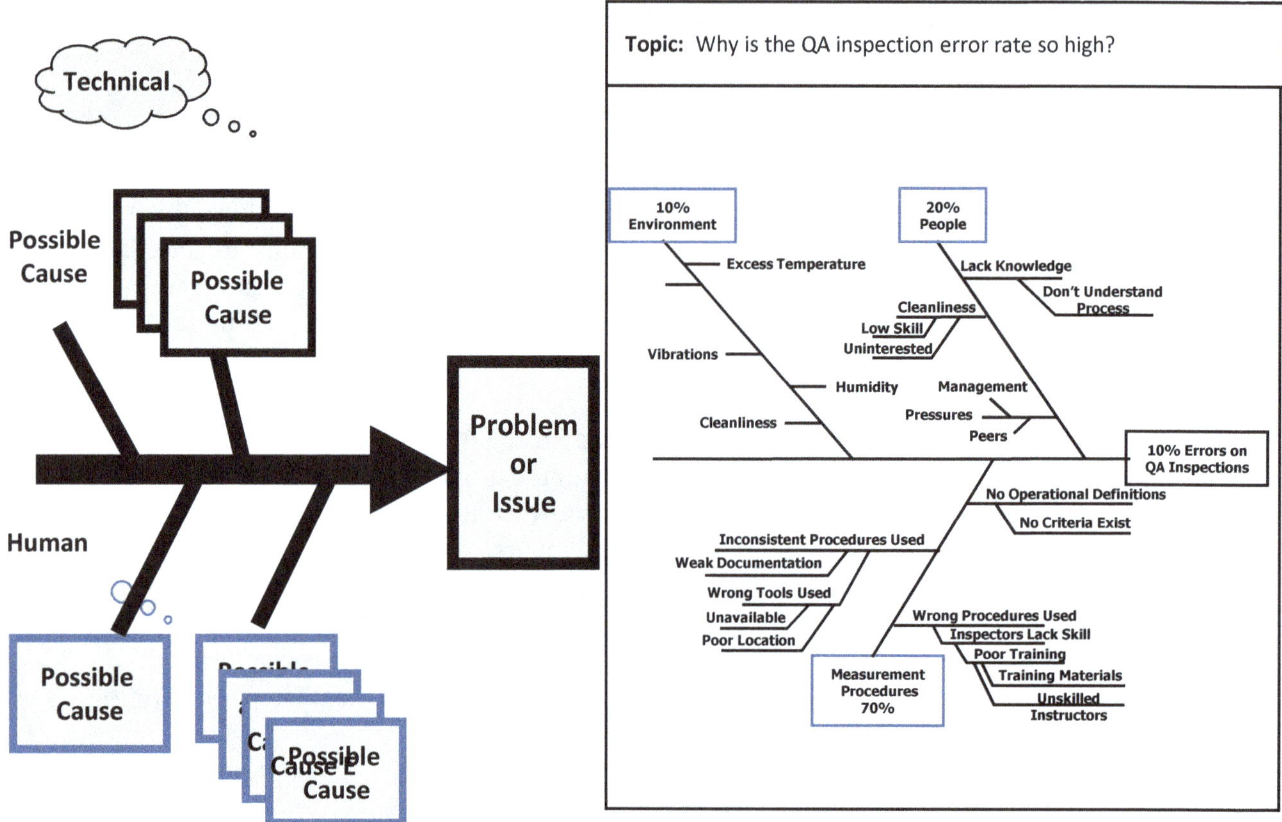

Pareto Principle

What is it?   **Pareto principle** is the 80/20 rule: 80% of all the problems are caused by 20% of all the sources (this is a rule of thumb, you can have a 60-30 Pareto, a 90-5 Pareto, etc.). Pareto Management can identify 'hidden' waste behind "chronic" problems, and help to separate "the vital few from the trivial many." Pareto charts are a special form of a bar chart used to display the relative importance of problems or conditions.

Why use it?   This tool is useful for deciding how best to deploy resources to work on problems:
1. Focuses on critical issues by ranking them in terms of importance and frequency
2. Establishes a priority to problems or causes to efficiently initiate problem solving
3. Supports analyzing problems or causes by different groupings of data, seeing trends & patterns
4. Supports analyzing the before and after impact of changes made in a process or system
5. Supports analyzing multiple metrics and revealing common failure modes in chronic problem areas

Steps:
1. Determine the categories of problems or causes to be compared. Begin by organizing the problems or causes into a narrowed down list of categories (usually 8 or less)
2. Select a standard unit of measurement and the time period to be studied. It could be a measure of how often something occurs (defects, errors, cost overruns, etc.); frequencies of reasons cited in surveys as the cause of a certain problem, or a specific measurement of volume or size. The time period to be studied should be a reasonable length of time to collect the data.
3. Collect and summarize the data. Create a three-column table with the headings of error or problem category, "frequency," and "percent of total." In the "error or problem category" list the categories of problems or causes previously identified. In the "frequency" column write in the totals for each of the categories over the designated period of time. In the "percent of Total" column, divide each number in the "frequency" column by the total number of measurements. This will provide the percentage of the total.
4. Plot the data that you have collected. One axis will be the categories of defects or problems in descending order with the most frequently occurring category on the far left or the top. The other axis will show the frequency for each of the categories.
5. Interpret your chart and find the pareto. Use common sense – just because a certain problem occurs most often doesn't necessarily mean it demands your greatest attention. You may want to create a more detailed pareto, after determining which problem category to address.

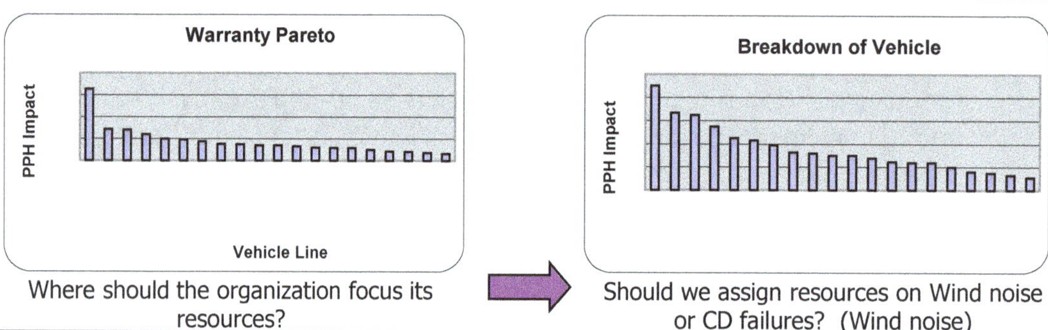

Where should the organization focus its resources?

Should we assign resources on Wind noise or CD failures? (Wind noise)

Tips:

1. Pareto Management is NOT fire fighting all known problems, but rather focusing effort on the few problems that hold the real value
2. Pareto Management allows you to identify what problems to work on in your area, department or organization, NOT what tool to use to fix it
3. Other tools will be used to solve these identified problems from Pareto Management based on the type of problem it is:
   - 7 Diamond Process: General observation tool (is it plugged in?)
   - Red X: Technical problem solving tool for 'hardy perennial' problems in product (quality, warranty, reliability) and manufacturing (process, operations, throughput)
   - VSM: Process flow tool used to identify areas of waste and apply to improve both mfg. and non-mfg. processes/value streams
   - 5S: Lean tool resulting in a clean, organized work area with standardized work and visual management
4. When it is important to leverage common resources across several organizations or locations, a more sophisticated method to determine the Pareto can be employed. Seek out statistical engineering expertise for support in doing this method.
   - Identify the business metrics and targets that need to be met, current status, and the gap.
   - Collect data showing how certain "problem areas" perform to the metric
   - Determine a % contribution to each metric for each problem area. This can be weighted for importance.
   - Determine the total % contribution for a "problem area" by adding up the % contribution from each metric.
   - Create and plot this ranking based on the total of the % contribution values.
   - Interpret the Pareto chart to comprehend total impact, rather than looking at the problem areas for each metric

Sample Pareto Chart when Using Multiple Metrics

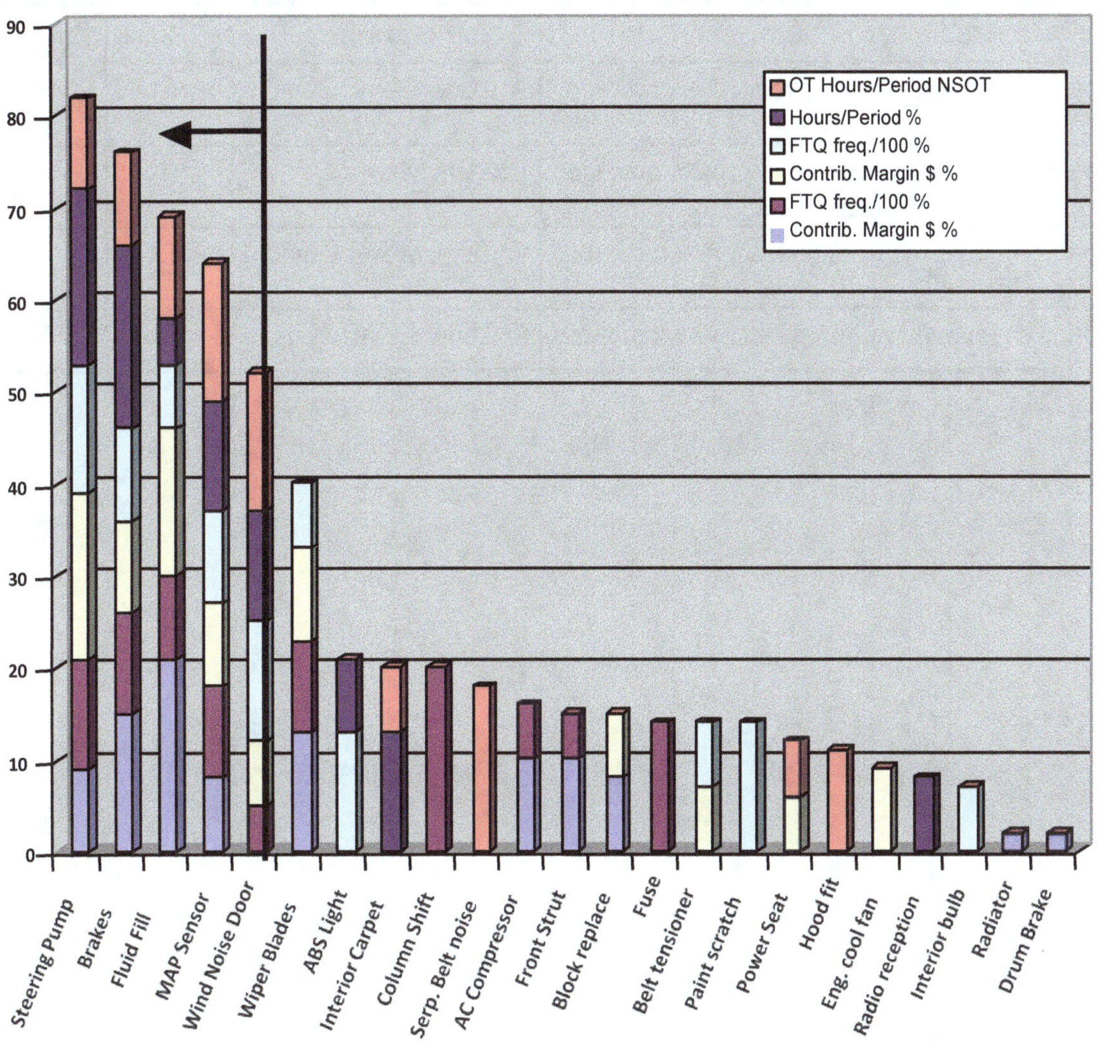

Working With Stakeholders/Participants

When you need to:	See this tool:	Page:
Identify stakeholders' attitudes related to proposed changes	Attitude Curve	63
Explore differences between good project manager behaviors and effective change leader behaviors	Leaders Matrix	65
Ensure the right participant and leader membership in a project	Participant and Leader Panel Lists	70
Determine the support required by key stakeholders	Stakeholder Analysis	74

Attitude Curve

What is it? **Attitude Curve** is used to classify stakeholders' likely attitudes towards the group's proposed changes; that is, who will be supportive or resistant and to what degree?

Why use it? The tool can:
1. Serve as a planning tool for implementing change
2. Help show the group the utility of "planning for the middle" rather than directing a disproportionate share of the group's energies and efforts towards resisters

Steps:
1. Determine which stakeholders (i.e., those that will impact the success of implementation efforts) are likely to be resisters
2. Identify which stakeholders, in addition to group members, are likely to be supportive (i.e., those that help develop the changes that will be implemented)
3. Divide the remaining stakeholders into the two middle categories
4. Develop strategies for engaging:
   a. Actively Supportive/ ++ Positives – Use these supporters to influence others
   b. Somewhat Supportive/ + Positives – Determine whether/how it's appropriate to involve them in implementing and/or "selling" the changes to key groups
   c. Somewhat Resistant/ - Negatives – Determine whether any additional efforts would be appropriate to move resisters to a more supportive position
   d. Actively Resistant/ -- Negatives – Determine cause of resistance; determine if they can be moved or how to contain their influence on other key stakeholders
5. Integrate outputs into an action plan

Tips:
1. By identifying the two ends of the attitude curve, it may be easier to classify the two middle groups
2. By first developing strategies for engaging the supporters, the group can determine whether they reduce the need for separate approaches for the other two classifications
3. Use to help identify where people fall related to the specific project – not in general
4. Use with the Stakeholder Analysis tool
5. Treat the results of this discussion as very confidential

Attitude Curve Tool

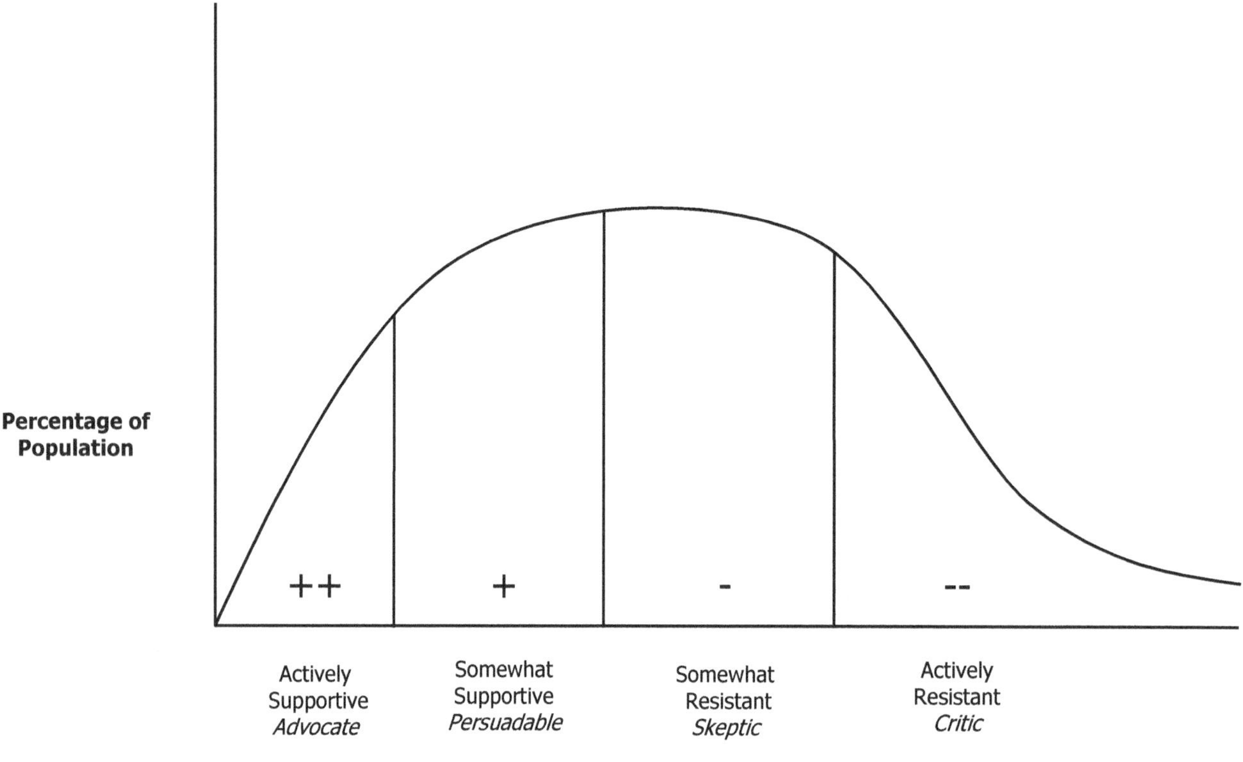

Leaders Matrix

What is it?   The **Leaders Matrix** explores the differences between what good project managers do and what effective change leaders do using an assessment matrix.

Why use it?   It provides:
1. A useful contrast of balance between project management (see Q work) and change leadership (see E work)
2. A framework for assessing leaders in order to plan for what needs to be done differently for the group's initiative

Steps:
1. Review the two pages that contrast what good project managers do and what effective change leaders do as a simple comparison presentation
2. Identify the leaders for the initiative and plot their current actions related to this project
3. Discuss where we need leaders to be compared to where they are today
4. Discuss the gaps and determine specific actions that should be incorporated into the group's action plan to strengthen the leadership provided for the initiative

Tips:
1. Consider broadening leaders for the initiative to include more than the group leader(s); e.g., include the project's sponsor(s) and/or champion and even the group members
2. In assessing tasks/skills/behaviors, consider using the axis as a continuum
3. If the group leader is uncomfortable with the group assessing his/her tasks/skills/behaviors or believes that the group members will be uncomfortable doing so, consider the value of generalizing steps 2 and 3 to the business unit's typical project/initiative management/leadership

Quality Solutions combined with Engagement Strategies

$$Q \quad x \quad E \quad = \quad T$$

Quality Solution through Project Management	Engagement through Change Leadership	Transformation
• Project defined • Strategy in place • Project leader and team appointed • Detailed master plans • Resources prioritised • Risk level assessed • Contingency plans in place • Tracking process in place	• Engagement, alignment, involvement and acceptance from all key stakeholders • Rationale communicated • Resistance anticipated and managed • Clear vision of future, goals, and accountabilities • Roadblocks identified and quickly addressed • Systems and processes changed to reinforce new ways of working	• Effective transformation is the product of rigorous project management AND engagement gained from involvement

Project Managers versus Change Leaders

An Investigation of Companies' Successful Change Initiatives Reveals the Critical Role of Change Leaders	
What Good Project Managers Do	**What Effective Change Leaders Do**
• State the objective of an initiative/project	• Frame and articulate a compelling and credible case for change • Communicate, communicate, communicate the change vision: in person, one-on-one and in groups; use symbols, metaphors, and stories to convey the vision • Set specific challenging (order-of-magnitude improvement) stretch goals
• Assign responsibility and delegate authority for steps of the project plan	• Stay involved, personally, and visibly • Discuss the change vision at every key meeting, in every resource allocation decision, business review, performance review, even in informal discussions
• Monitor and review progress in executing the project plan	• Recognize successes frequently, especially in public forums • Remain persistent, consistent, and always optimistic in support and advocacy ("failure is not an option")

Project Managers versus Change Leaders

An Investigation of Companies' Successful Change Initiatives Reveals the Critical Role of Change Leaders	
What Good Project Managers Do	**What Effective Change Leaders Do**
• Develop a process to address variances in the implementation plan	• Successfully influence and persuade others to become advocates and leaders of the change
• Request and focus on potential solutions that are consistent with desired objectives	• Alter the metrics that define success • Hold his/her team/leaders accountable for implementing, not just designing, solutions
• Patiently allow the project to operate	• Impatiently reiterate the need for decisive action; make speed a top priority
• Focus on project tasks, activities and timetables	• Focus on resistant sources and accurately assess the degree of resistance • Build necessary coalitions needed to effect change
• Emphasize project outcomes	• Emphasize altering the organization's performance

Project Managers versus Change Leaders

An Investigation of Companies' Successful Change Initiatives Reveals the Critical Role of Change Leaders	
What Good Project Managers Do	**What Effective Change Leaders Do**

What Good Project Managers Do

- Develop a process to address variances in the implementation plan

- Request and focus on potential solutions that are consistent with desired objectives

- Patiently allow the project to operate

- Focus on project tasks, activities and timetables

- Emphasize project outcomes

What Effective Change Leaders Do

- Successfully influence and persuade others to become advocates and leaders of the change

- Alter the metrics that define success

- Hold his/her team/leaders accountable for implementing, not just designing, solutions

- Impatiently reiterate the need for decisive action; make speed a top priority

- Focus on resistant sources and accurately assess the degree of resistance

- Build necessary coalitions needed to effect change

- Emphasize altering the organization's performance

Participant and Leadership Panel Lists

What is it? The **Participant List and Leadership Panel List** ensure the "right" participants and leadership panel members are included in a process-improvement project (e.g. value stream). Both tools ensure participants and leadership are involved from 3 areas of the process: 1) Supplier of the Process; 2) Operator of the Process; and 3) Customer of the Process.

Why use it?
1. Supports the waste element "People Involvement," the essential ingredient in creating a world class organization.
2. Ensures the right leadership panels members are included in process improvement projects
   - Builds ownership in business processes and results
   - Identifies processes with no single leader/shared leadership
   - Identifies the need for cross-functional improvement
   - Helps drive accountability
3. Ensures the right participants are included in process improvement projects
   - Builds ownership in business processes and results
   - Those closest to the work are best able to improve the work
   - Drives approval and implementation to the lowest level of the organization
   - Drives cross-functional participation for the improvement of the whole

Steps: The following steps are normally performed during the scoping phase of a project:
1. Identify the customer(s) of the process and the customer's expectations
2. Use the SIPOC tool to identify and make visual the high level process which includes **S**upplier(s), **I**nputs, **P**rocess steps, **O**utputs, and **C**ustomer(s).
3. Gain agreement on the SIPOC from group members
4. Use the Leadership Panel List to document names of leadership panel members from each category of the process (Suppliers, Operators, and Customers)
   - Majority should come from "Operates the Process."
5. Use the Participant List to document names of participants from each category of the process (Suppliers, Operators & Customers)
   - Majority should come from "Operates the Process"
6. Continue to review and update the Leadership Panel Tool and the Participant Tool during future scoping session
7. Ensure final lists of names are approved by the Sponsor, Leadership Panel, and scoping participants

Leadership Panel List:

Tips:

1. Ask "Who needs to give approval or provide resources to ensure implementation?"
2. Ask "Who could prevent implementation if not involved?"
3. Remember to ask about less obvious organizations. Ask "What about support organizations like Quality, IS & S, Legal, Outside Suppliers, etc.?"
4. Make sure the Sponsor(s) of the project is(are) in agreement with the names on the Leadership Panel List; Make sure the scoping participants also agree with the list.

Participant List: (can be used to define scoping participants or workshop participants)

1. Ask for those people who know most about the process and are capable of implementing the change
2. Ask for those people that if excluded could prevent successful implementation
3. Include people that want to see the process improved
4. Make sure all participants in the scoping sessions as well as the Leadership Panel agree on the final Participant List

Leadership Panel List Tool

Supplies Info to the Process	Operates the Process	Customers of the Process

Majority of Leadership Panel Members should come from this section.

Participant List Tool

Supplies Info to the Process	Operates the Process	Customers of the Process

Majority of the Participants
should come from this section.

Stakeholder Analysis

What is it?   The **Stakeholder Analysis** provides a framework to determine the support required by key stakeholders.

Why use it?   The Stakeholder Analysis helps the group identify for every key stakeholder:

1. Their likely position regarding the group's solution (i.e., supportive or resistant)
2. The degree of support needed from the key stakeholder to have a reasonable or good probability of successful implementation of the changes
3. The most critical gaps between where stakeholder support is needed and where it exists
4. The plan for closing the gaps

Steps:

1. Brainstorm the list of possible stakeholders
2. Select the key stakeholders
3. For each *key* stakeholder, determine their likely position regarding the proposed changes; i.e., whether they are likely to be very supportive/positive (++), generally supportive (+), somewhat resistant (-), or very resistant (--)
4. Draw an X to note their current position
5. Discuss the reasons for their current position
6. For each *key* stakeholder, identify the degree of support needed to enable successful implementation of desired changes — draw an O to note the needed position — and draw an arrow connecting the X and O for each stakeholder
7. Discuss and note the key actions that are likely to be required to shift key stakeholders' positions
8. Identify influencing strategies and action plans for the most important stakeholders

Tips:

1. This tool is most powerful when used to gain insight into individual stakeholders
2. Encourage the group not to get too distracted by the incremental ratings — they are meant only as a rough approximation of a position; i.e., whether a key stakeholder is somewhat resistant or actively resistant is less important than where they need to be and how the group plans on moving them there
3. Determine which stakeholders are likely to influence the position of other stakeholders (for example, if a business unit's executive committee is a key stakeholder, their position may sway other stakeholders that are subordinate in the organizational hierarchy — not by asserting hierarchical control, but

by helping persuade reluctant stakeholders)
4. Remind the group that not all key stakeholders need to be ++ or actively supportive
5. Based on the above tip, determine if there is a logical order/sequence to any actions that are identified for shifting key stakeholders' positions
6. Suggest the group treat this analysis as confidential and not share or present the results outside of this group

Stakeholder Analysis Tool

Instructions:

1. Identify all stakeholders as specifically as possible on a separate sheet
2. Identify the key stakeholders and list on the table
3. Identify your perception of their current position regarding the initiative and mark with an X
4. Discuss their reasons for current position
5. Identify the position they need to be, mark with an O and draw an arrow to that column
6. Identify actions are required to influence key stakeholders to alter their position

Key Stakeholders[1]	++	+	-	--	Stakeholders' Position on the Initiative
					Reasons for Current Position; Actions Required to Alter Position

Note: (1) Individuals, teams, units, positions

Stakeholder Analysis - Influencing Strategies Tool

Instructions:

1. List the key stakeholders that need to be influenced
2. Identify each stakeholder's issues and concerns with the initiative
3. Identify "wins" each stakeholder can gain out of this initiative

Stakeholder	Issues/Concerns	Identify Strategies	Identify Action Steps

Working With Action Items/Implementation

When you need to:	See this tool:	Page:
Capture ideas requiring action and ensure accountability for completion of actions	Action Register	78
Think through the who, what, what, why, how and when of messages to be communicated	Communications Action Plan	81
Analyze, design or re-design responsibilities and accountabilities	RASIC	83
Document standardized work for non-manufacturing processes	SOS and JES for Non-Manufacturing Processes	86

Action Register

What is it?   The **Action Register** is used to capture ideas as they are presented in meetings so they are not overlooked or lost. It is a basic accountability tool that captures the task to be completed, who is responsible for completing the task and the expected date of completion. The action register is reviewed in each meeting to ensure compliance to the deliverables expected by the group from prior meetings and to agree on new, future deliverables from the current meeting. It also serves as a historic tool for task completion.

Why use it?   This tool is useful whenever one or more employees gather for a meeting. The action register:

1. Increases the effectiveness of meetings by documenting ideas requiring action
2. Ensures everyone in the meeting has the same understanding of actions to be taken
3. Establishes single point accountability with an expected delivery date for all tasks
4. Establishes a record of both open items and closed items for repetitive meetings
5. Enhances communication and recognition between team members

Steps:

1. Develop a simple spreadsheet with the headings: Action, Responsibility, Target Date, Complete Date, ✓ , and comments (optional field for information or retiming)
2. Ensure the action register is an agenda item at the end of each meeting
   - Optional: Cover open items at the beginning of the meeting and new items at the end of the meeting
3. When using the action register during a meeting:
   - Review the use and rules of the action register with meeting attendees, as required
   - Review and check off closed-out items (for communication, recognition and accountability)
   - List new steps to achieve actions
   - Designate who is responsible for each step
   - Ask the person responsible for each step for a target date
   - Gain approval/commitment from the entire team on all open items
4. Publish action register, reminding owners to record completion dates as items are completed and to give advance notice if a target date cannot be met

Tips:

1. A meeting is usually more effective if the facilitator of the meeting does not have the responsibility for the action register
2. Never assign tasks to absent members
3. Only place "one" name in the responsibility column even if more than one person is working on the task and establishes one contact point
4. Rotate the responsibility for the action register (e.g. monthly)
5. Ensure the action register is accessible to all participants (e.g. share drive) to allow team members to update their complete dates and/or add comments
6. Ensure specific target dates are used - ASAP is not an acceptable target date to ensure completion of tasks
7. If a target date gets changed, the original date should not be deleted, just crossed out with a new date placed above the original date or the new date and reason reflected in the "comments" field to prevent tasks from continually being re-timed due to lack of completion
8. Use the checkmark field to communicate the completion of tasks and to attain consensus from the group that the task has been completed
9. Use completed tasks as an opportunity to recognize people for a task well-done
10. Do not leave the meeting until an owner has been designated and a date for completion has been set
11. Ensure there is always time allotted on the agenda for the review of the action register or it will lose its effectiveness

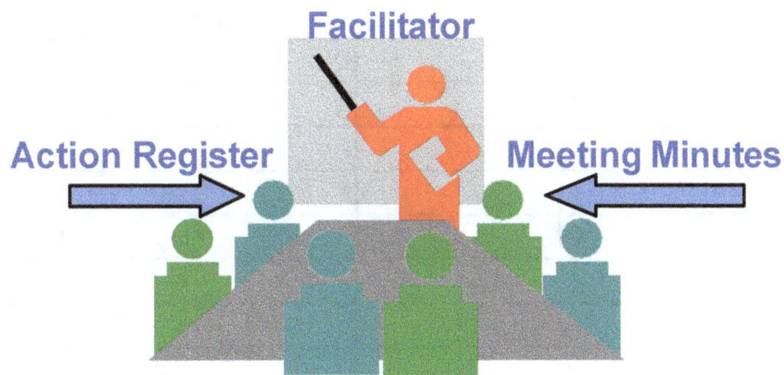

Action Register Tool

Actions = WHAT

Responsibility = WHO

Target Date = WHEN

Name of Meeting

ACTION	RESPONSIBILITY (One Name)	TARGET DATE	COMPLETE DATE	✓	COMMENTS
				·	
				·	
				·	
				·	
				·	
				·	
				·	
				·	

Note : Place a ✓ in the far right column to indicate completed item has been reviewed.

Communications Action Plan

What is it? **Communications Action Plan** provides groups with a framework for thinking through the who, what, why, how, and when of any messages that need to be communicated.

Why use it? Communications Action Plan helps groups consider how to use communication efforts to help successfully implement their desired changes:
1. Identify the audience
2. Identify the content of the messages to be communicated
3. Determine the objective of the communication
4. Consider the best approach or method for communicating the content and objective
5. Define the communications timing

Steps:
1. Identify all relevant stakeholders who need to be kept informed
2. For each audience answer the what/why/how/when questions
3. Incorporate the necessary communication activities/milestones defined here into a action plan

Tips:
1. Whenever others outside the immediate group need to be informed, persuaded, or involved, use the communications action plan framework to determine the best approach
2. Consider:
    a. To whom the message should be directed
    b. What the message should be to each audience — the message may be somewhat different to distinct groups since their concerns/issues may be different
    c. If group members are not sure of what the likely concerns of a given audience group are likely to be, then they should try and find that out before crafting the message
    d. What the objective of the message is, and what the most relevant channel is; this may differ by audience
3. Integrate communication action plan items into the group's overall action plan

Communications Action Plan Tool

<table>
<tr><td>Instructions:</td></tr>
</table>

1. Identify *all* relevant players/stakeholders who need to be kept informed
2. For each audience answer the What/Why/How/When questions
3. Incorporate the necessary communication activities/milestones into project work plans

Who?	What?	Why?	How?	When?
• Audience(s) who need to receive information • Communicators who will send/initiate the communications	• Concise, compelling statement of the initiative and its outcomes • Content of the communication	• Rationale, impact, and priority for the initiative	• Methods/channels used to communicate	• Schedule/ timeframe for communications

RASIC

What is it?   **Responsible, Authority, Support, Inform, Consult (RASIC)** is used for analyzing, designing, or re-designing responsibilities and accountabilities for processes and/or key decisions.

Why use it? RASIC can help groups:

1. Identify unclear, overlapping, redundant, or inconsistent responsibility and levels of authority for processes and/or key decisions
2. Examine inefficiencies in the way an organization structure distributes responsibility and authority
3. Design or re-design clear responsibility and authority for processes and key decisions

Steps:

1. Clarify the decision or process that is being analyzed, designed, or re-designed
2. Complete the left-hand column of the tool (i.e., Key Decisions or Process Steps)
3. Identify those involved in the decision or process under consideration, and complete the column headings with either position, function, or unit (usually identifying a position is better than an individual, unless a responsibility lies with a group such as an executive committee, or a product-planning group)
4. Complete each cell, identifying those that are responsible (**R**), have approval authority (**A**), supports a step (**S**), is informed (**I**), or is consulted (**C**) for each decision or process step

Guidelines for designing/re-designing a process/decision:

- Only designate one **R** for each decision or step
- The **R** should be assigned to a position, rather than a committee
- Designate an **A** only if necessary; not all steps or decisions may require an **A**
- Ensure that appropriate **S, I, C** are designated, but keep it to necessary involvement only

Analyzing a current process/decision:

1. If there are multiple **R**s or **A**s for a step or a decision, note them
2. Multiple **R**s or **A**s may be either because there are different views of responsibilities and approvals, or because there actually are multiple **R**s or **A**s
3. Be sure to capture all those involved with responsibilities for **S, I, C** since if some of these are not needed in an improved process they will have to be notified of a change

Tips:

1. RASIC is a useful complement to a process map, since it can get into more detailed responsibilities than the typical process map
2. Think of a process map at one level of abstraction and RASIC as the next level of detail
3. If a process or key decision is being re-designed or improved, RASIC can be very useful in identifying improvements needed
4. In analyzing, designing, or re-designing a process, consider the benefits of pushing responsibilities down — i.e., increasing the level of responsibility from an **S** to an **R**, and an **R** to an **A** (if an **A** is needed at all)
5. Be sure to complete a RASIC with those that are either involved in a process or decision, or with those that are very familiar with that process or decision; this tends to reduce the chances of omissions or inaccuracies

RASIC Tool

Instructions:	Guidelines:
1. Identify/list key decisions or process steps 2. Identify/list all individuals/groups involved 3. Complete the matrix by assigning **R/A/S/I/C** as appropriate	• Only one **R** allowed per decision/step • Multiple **A**s are discouraged — a **S** might be more appropriate • **R/A** is the only combination allowed

R — Responsible (Takes lead on)[1]
A — Approve (Final decision) **S** — Supports (Actively assists) **I** — Informed (Made aware)
C — Consulted (Provides advice)

Key Decisions or Process Steps	**Individuals/Stakeholders/Roles**						
• Decision/Step #1							
• Decision/Step #2							
• Decision/Step #3							

Note: (1) Only one **R** per decision

SOS and JES for Non-manufacturing Processes

What is it? **Standard Operation Sheets (SOS) and Job Element Sheets (JES)** are the globally approved forms used to document Standardized Work. The SOS is a document that organizes job elements into a sequence that can be successfully repeated. The JES is a user friendly document that provides detailed information on a specific element of work to ensure the successful execution of that element.

Why use it? The SOS illustrates the flow of work for a complete operation. The JES provides more detail indicating Key Points (how) and Reasons (why) elements must be completed. Both documents can be used for training new team members, analyzing jobs for improvement opportunity, auditing, and problem solving.

Steps:
1. List all the major elements of work on the SOS
2. Fill in the header information
3. Use the diagram area for pictures, flow charts, or Value Stream Maps
4. Complete a JES for each work element listed on the SOS
5. Fill in the header information
6. Enter the first Major Step (What), the Key Point (How), and the Reason (Why)
7. Repeat step 6 for each Major Step
8. Use symbols by each Major Step to identify safety cautions, mandatory sequences, and quality checks
9. Use the diagram area for specific reference to a Major Step. For example, hyperlinks, forms, reference documents, pictures, etc.

Tips:
1. The people who know the jobs best should be responsible for the creation, maintenance, and improvement of Standardized Work
2. Standardized Work should be posted and up-to-date
3. Managers should audit Standardized Work to ensure adherence
4. Use when there is a definable, repeatable process
5. Use as a baseline for Continuous Improvement

Index

Sources

Carreira, B. Lean Manufacturing that Works: Powerful Tools for dramatically Reducing Waste and Maximizing Profits. Nov 19, 2004.

Gray, A. Business Development Body of Knowledge (BD-BOK): Business Development Professional (BDP) Certification Handbook Paperback – January 30, 2023

Kendrick, T. The Project Management Tool Kit: 100 Tips and Techniques for Getting the Job Done Right. Dec 19, 2013

Silberman, M. (Editor), *The Consultant's Big Book of Organization Development Tools*, McGraw Hill; 1st edition December 11, 2002